UnTimed:

Why Time Management is a waste of your time and what your Options are-

A Guide to Personal Productivity.

Nii Boi-Dsane

Copyright © 2020 by Nii Boi-Dsane

All rights reserved

This book is the bona fide intellectual property of the author and copyright holder. Please, support the writing industry; respect the fact and do not participate in or encourage the unauthorized use of copyrighted material.

It is not permitted to reproduce any part of this material in any form, or by any means, be it graphic, electronic, or mechanical, including, but not limited to, distribution whether in whole or any part thereof via the internet or other means, photocopying, scanning, recording, taping, or by any system of information storage or retrieval, without the express written permission of the author and publisher.

Strenuous attempts have been made to credit all copyrighted materials used in this book. All such materials and trademarks, which are referenced in this book, are the full property of their respective copyright owners. It must be affirmed that this writer has no relationship, business or otherwise, with any of the copyright holders, and this work has neither been endorsed by any such, nor has such an endorsement been sought, except where expressly stated otherwise. Every effort has been made to obtain copyright permission for material quoted in this book. Any omissions will be rectified in future editions.

The material in this book is made available on an "as is" basis, and sans warranty of any kind. This book does not contain professional advice. The contents are not meant to replace professional advice and may not be relied on in lieu of such professional advice. For professional advice relating to any part of the book, please consult an appropriate and suitably qualified professional. This book with its contents is used subject to the understanding that on no occasion shall either the author or publisher have any liability whatsoever to any entity or person in respect of any loss or damage caused or otherwise alleged to be caused whether directly or indirectly in connection with this book and its contents.

Finally, even though every effort has been made to ensure the accuracy of the contents of this book, it is recognized that errors and omissions can still occur. Should this be the case, apologies are in order, and the author accepts full responsibility. These will be corrected in subsequent revisions.

Dedication

I dedicate this work to my children, Kofi and Naa, who bore the consequences of my decisions, suffered from the tailwind of my choices, and those imposed on me. The labour was yours too.

Acknowledgements

I thank Paulina Duker for reading the first draft and providing useful feedback.

To Jane Dawson, thank you for your advice regarding publishing options and for sharing your professional experiences with me.

Our difficulty with Time is not the managing; nor is it the requirement for self-discipline relative to time itself. The greater task lies in our ability to manage our self-management such that it enables us a more purposeful utilization of time as a resource.

From Untimed

Table of Contents

Dedication 4
Acknowledgements 4
Introduction 9
The purpose of this book 12
Why did I write this book? 13

Chapter One **15**
The Time Equation: A history of time 15
Time Management as we know it. 16

Chapter Two **22**
What does "time" mean to you? 22
Time as individually determined, but also a socio-cultural construct 24
Of Personal Individual Time: 26
Time as Socially Determined 29
Of Time in small packages: The Four Seasons. .. 32
Time and productivity 37
Time Management: An Assessment Exercise. ... 40

Chapter Three **44**
Leveraging for Productivity. 44

The Power of Leverage: 45

Leverage through the ages: 45

Leveraging as the modern wealth genie: 49

Exercise: My Personal leverage tools. 52

Leveraging and the self: 53

The Art of Prioritization 55

Chapter Four **57**

Self-Management and Time: What Relationship? 57

Managing for Self-Management 58

The Power of the Will 63

The Time Audit: 67

Making Magic normal. 68

Stolen Time: The scourge of the social media apparatus. 71

Chapter Five **76**

A shifting of the Paradigm: On doing things differently, and the rewards of learning from others. 76

Mastering your 1440 78

Planning for joy 79

Why the 8-hour workday doesn't work. 82

The Virtue of Having a Personal Daily Ritual: 85

Chapter Six **88**
What's left? 88
The Virtue of Building Strategic Relationships 95
On showing up with your whole self 96

Chapter Seven **99**
And Finally: 99
In praise of self-care: Time Management and your health 100

Introduction

If you do not know how to live, look to nature. -NB-D

Time management is a waste of your time. I said so. If you don't agree, make my day, go on and disappoint yourself.

Go on, grab a drink, make yourself comfortable, read on, and I will show you why. You would be better off. I promise you. Great! Come along, say your prayers because the only way we can WIN against *Time* is to lose the time management game you and I have been playing for so long.

Let me ask you this: How can one manage an entity one has no control over? Trying to manage what we call "time", is like taking on a responsibility without the power to execute it. How effective is that?

No doubt, *Time* is the essence of being, for without it, we are not; and when we are not, nothing is. What do we care about the boast of eternity? Nothing. It is in the here and now, that time offers us a chance to be significant and if we choose our song suitably and choreograph our routine appropriately, we will see that our dance with time cannot but be a feast of fruitful delight.

The point here is that, it is what we choose to do with time in our moments of engagement that matters, and not how we *strive to harness it*. Hear this:

Our difficulty with Time is not the managing; nor is it the requirement for self-discipline relative to time itself. The greater task lies in our ability to manage our self-management

such that it enables us a more purposeful utilization of time as a resource.

This is the premise of this book. In my view, time "management", is all about moments, captured; minutes and seconds secured in the reward of work well-done, as well as the satisfaction of necessary action duly executed, noble plans set on course and energy and skill applied to good ends. I dare argue, that rather than thinking to "manage" time, we can only capture the essence of time through our proper application of it. Therefore, instead of seeking to "manage" time how about we begin honouring it. We honour time by showing respect in our use of it to achieve aims more worthy, more noble, more in line with our best selves, our dreams, our desires; those things we mean to bring to fruition, those heights we mean to, and know we can attain, if only we apply ourselves in the moments we have.

There has been a lot of work done regarding time and productivity over the years. However, of late, with our ever-increasing drive for productivity, this issue has become even more relevant as time seems to have become more and more "scarce", and therefore, more valuable. Time is a commodity like all else. We trade it all the time. In fact, for all our talk of work and remuneration et cetera, all we are really doing is selling our time for a bit of profit. Those who have managed to make their time more valuable in the arena of the work enterprise than others get rewarded correspondingly more.

In short, if you desire more out of time, make yours all the more valuable. It is only fair. For starters, a unit of my time, of your time, of his time and of her time are not of the same value. Indeed, they cannot be for we come to the market place with different skills, offerings and benefits relative to societal demands and what the market-place values in both relative and real terms. The economics of time is however, beyond the scope of this book.

In life, everything is about perspective. I would argue that the problem we seem to have with time is not the problem of time but with our relationship with it. Urgency may prompt more adrenal rush and busyNESS, but it's mastery and control of the self, relative to the resource of time that ultimately wins the day. It's the way it is. There is no other outcome; never has been, and never will be. Master time, and all else shall fall in place. But to master time, we must first master the self. "Why?" you ask? Simple. It is because, time is "us".

Yes, you are all there is to time. Your time is you. If Time is "us" it would follow then, that if we can manage ourselves, then and only then can we begin to win at the game of time. Self-acknowledgement and self-knowledge through appropriate and unfiltered introspection is the starting point, to "healing" our relationship with Time.

This is the focus of the endeavour at hand, and the primary purpose of this book:

Untimed-Why time management is a waste of your time, and what your options are- A Guide to Personal Productivity.

Let's explore the various arguments as to why time management is indeed a waste of your time, in the chapters that follow.

The purpose of this book.

What it is not: This book is not a prescription of what to do. It is not an advocacy against time management per se for what it is in the traditional sense, nor is it a cry of nothingness over an equally "nothing- can- be done- situation".

The purpose is to encourage, to prompt, to engender meaningful reflection, a dialogue with the self, regarding (y)our relationship with "time"; to question why (you) we have allowed (yourself) ourselves to be unquestioningly ruled by something (you) we have the resources to master, but have perhaps failed or neglected to.

It is meant as a sort of prompt, a wake-up call to the realisation that there has to be a better way of dealing with time and productivity in our lives, individually and collectively; that if we are to be truly productive, we need to free ourselves from the shackles and tyranny of time; that we need to in effect "un-time" ourselves not by ignoring time as it were, no, but by mastering it through an essential mastery of ourselves, gaining control of who we are, and our purposes, for our task is not to manage time, but to "un-time" ourselves and to remove all the barriers we have set up against our proper utilisation of that resource.

Why did I write this book?

To the ill-prepared, time is a mere footnote in the day, with nothing special to offer; to the well-organized, time is the most valuable, trusted and worthy of all that the day bestows, a potent force for the realization of life's mission and goals, one small step at a time. –NB-D

The idea for this book arose during my research for *Retire Well: A guide to what is important in retirement-Health, Wealth and Relationships*, published by Librotas Books. A big part of retirement life is the issue of time. In some cases, time becomes suddenly abundant almost overnight, and what to do with it or, if you like, how to "manage" it becomes a problem in and of itself.

For most of our working lives, a lot of us rarely have to encounter time as an abundant entity on our hands begging for utility. Our everyday busyNESS with work and home life leaves little room for such considerations. Yet, confronted with an abundance of time, such as the world experienced during the height of the global pandemic of 2020, courtesy of the COVID-19 virus, we know that it is in such a situation that one becomes alerted to the weighty imposition of what it means to have "time"; what time may be; its nature; its essence; its utility or not; and thus perhaps to begin to understand what it means to have; to suffer; even to endure the company of time and how to "manage" it.

On the other hand, I have also worked with clients whose biggest head ache is that there doesn't seem to be enough "time" in the day to get "it all" done, whatever "it all" mean be.

But we need to calm down, for time can be a friend. It may sound easy. It is not, for it is in the very nature of time that it seems to cease to acquiesce to our wishes the moment we begin to monitor it. Try missing a train for an important event and waiting for the next one. You know that feeling of having to wait forever? Yep! That is time for you. It does slow down when you would have it pass faster.

At the very core of the concept of time management is the desire for productivity. Given the experiences outlined above, I have been thinking about our human relationship with time; what we mean when we talk "Time management"; how we manifest the same, whether there could be or, there are other less transactional, more wholesome, more "celebratory" ways of relating to and honouring time to achieve our productive ends. There is an argument to the effect that the answer is indeed, "yes". Productivity is less about time management per se, and more about a management of the self, relative to time use. We shall see "why" in due course. But what is "time", and how did we come to concern ourselves with the notion of time. That is the subject of our next section.

Chapter One

"Time is too slow for those who wait, too swift for those who fear, too long for those who grieve, too short for those who rejoice, but for those who love, time is eternity". – Henry van Dyke Jr.

The Time Equation: A history of time

Scientists are united in their belief that the universe began with a big bang, "The big bang" as it is called. However, no one has come up with what was before the big bang even though by scientific notions, nothing arises out of a vacuum. I guess there's no knowing of everything, and not everything requires an explanation. Some things are just a mystery and a mystery they must remain. Well, we will stick with what is. Time began with the big bang, end of the story. It is also said to be impersonal. It also exists in all cultures. However, in some cases, time exists not as we may know or think it is.

Well, what about you and I? How did time begin for us? It is arguable that our time began at conception, or perhaps when we ultimately saw the sun, our moment of birth. It all depends on our individual beliefs regarding when life begins. You are free to choose yours, dear reader. For me, it makes absolutely no difference so long as it is valid for you. So, whatever we choose to belief, that was when time began for us individually. How democratic! Of course, we knew nothing about the concept of time then. Even now, what we know, we have gleaned from our social and cultural contexts, orientations and interactions.

Curiously however, we all tend to think our idea of time is the definitive. Many of us hardly ever stop to question why we view time the way we do.

The truth however, is that time is fundamentally relative, according to the experts. Additionally, it is also not only a matter of perspective, but crucially, it is subjective. Only the display on that timepiece you and I so religiously consult may be objective. Even this, is largely… relative. Yep! It is for this reason that we have Greenwich Mean Time, United Time Coordinated, Eastern Time, Pacific Time and so on. These are calculated with reference to some other measure. There is no absolute time. One time zone is only valid as it relates to another. After all the International Date Line is man-made. Is it not?

It passes through Greenwich in London, and runs southwards through Tema, in Ghana, West Africa and further down through the Atlantic Ocean. But could it well have been associated with Moscow, or Tokyo, New Delhi or Singapore, perhaps? Well, not exactly. Scientific calculations back up where the so-called Longitude "0" is. So, yes, time may be relative but as we are beginning to discover, there's a basis for its relativity. Importantly, it is from this basis that all experience of time derives.

Time Management as we know it.

Time management has generally been defined as the ability to use time as a resource productively and with efficiency in order to do one's work or attain a desired outcome. The idea here is that time management is the key to achieving productivity. Well, this is our traditional notion of what the subject is. Everyone or nearly everyone gets this. But you and I are not everyone. We are "you" and "I". Are you smiling? That is good. It means you know you are unique. Haha! If this notion of time management was all there was to productivity, then we should all be productive indeed, for being the adherents we are and have been to this understanding. But we are not.

The key phrase in the definition is "productively and with efficiency". Some people are more productive with their 24 hours than others. So, the question is: what does time management mean to you? Indeed, we must seek a different path from the rest if we are not to end up like everyone else, for if we approach the subject like everyone else, then we will inevitably end up of course like everyone else. When it comes to time and its role in productivity, a lot of us get disappointed, because of course there is more to productivity than we sometimes acknowledge. Given this, what then, is the essence of time management, and how should one approach the practice?

This to me comes down to seeing to our time needs before our time wants. In other words, do not violate the spirit of Maslow's hierarchy of needs. There are tasks that the security of your being is based on. Do what needs to be done before what you may want done. It's about effectiveness first, and always. In the section that follows, we shall discuss some "tried and tested" useful principles for harnessing our time more productively.

Here we go:
- **Planning to plan.**

This may seem obvious. It may be. But it is also a most vital habit to acquire and develop. Yes, you read it right. Plan to plan. Be intentional about what you want; make it a priority and set aside creative thinking time to analyse and develop a road map or a series of steps for achieving your ends. Some time ago, I found myself out of a major long-standing contract. It was also the very first time in many years that I realised I was able to set aside time to think properly and to creatively find solutions to many key projects that I had been grappling with. It was an eye-opener.

One particular issue I had been "throwing" money at was resolved, not with money, but with creative thinking. You see, I had been suffering from neck pain. I had been to see the specialists and machines had had their say. I was spending quite a bit on physical therapy. Nothing worked. With no longer the need to wake up and rush to complete tasks to beat a deadline, I re-arranged my morning routine to include "thinking time". It was a revelation. Before bedtime each night, I would write down and plan what I was going to "creatively" tackle in the morning.

One morning, I had an insight. I stopped sitting at my usual desk and decided to stand when working. That was the solution money couldn't buy. I am pain-free now. My posture was the culprit. So, yes, planning to plan and setting time aside to think creatively can and does yield results.

- **Hunt for elephants, first and then ants.** Organisation and prioritization of need-to-do tasks and want-to-do-tasks is paramount, indeed.

It would seem self-explanatory, but it can be tricky, because our wants tend to be loud and very good at grabbing our attention. Do beware.

- **Applying The Pareto principle (The 80/20 Rule).**

This rule was made famous by an Italian economist, of the same name. The claim is that, 80 portions of our success in whatever area of endeavour come from 20 portions of our efforts. It is said that a farmer once observed that 80 percent of his yield came from only 20 percent of the land. This is where the economist is said to have had the idea. It is apparent in all areas of life. If 20% of your activities yield 80% of your income, then you would be wise indeed to concentrate on those 20% of activities. Think about it. Simply put, success does not require perfection of anyone; only that we know what our 20% is and to focus on it. It can't be that difficult. Can it? Well, it takes planning and execution.

- **Multi-tasking is dead. -The virtue of Doing- One-Thing- At- A- Time.**

Multi-tasking used to be hailed as the king of productivity. Now we know better. One thing-at-a-time done well indeed, does it.

- **Be completely selfish with your productive time (Kill Distractions and interruptions).**

Do not allow others to use up your productive time and energies. It is up to you…and oh! There's absolutely no need to feel guilty about protecting your time. It is your life.

- **Know that you cannot do it all.**

    Your time is valuable. Put a price on it. If the task at hand cannot adequately compensate for the time you have to spend on it, DELEGATE it. That is how you show you value your time, and once you get to know the true value of your time, it becomes easy to delegate. Everybody wins, because the delegatee gets to do work that otherwise might be out of reach and in so doing builds capacity. Do you see how a simple task delegation can have added value for your team?

- **"Don't Worry, Be Happy".**

    It is the title of a popular song. Worry never solves any problem. It only serves to cloud judgment, stress us, and make us prone to avoidable mistakes. It sounds easy. It is not. But it is worth remembering and endeavouring to practise not worrying.

- **Know when "NO" is the only appropriate answer.**

    Warren Buffet, one of the very finest investment and business minds ever to pass this place we call home for now, is reputed to have once said that the difference between successful and VERY successful people is that VERY successful people have learnt to say "NO" to most things. Think about it.

    Now, please do me a favour. Please go back and re-read the above. What did you notice? Do you see how all these techniques and principles of time management have very little to do with time and absolutely everything to do with the SELF? The question then is: what does time management mean to you? This is the basis of our discussion in the next section.

Time is precious; time is fleeting; time is short, we cry. Yet… our task is not to manage time; it is to remove all the barriers we have built up against our proper utilization and enjoyment of it."- (In honour of Rumi)

Chapter Two

What does "time" mean to you?

No matter what we make of it, Time is "us". Time is life itself, so when we focus on time and attempt to control or "manage" it as if it is some sort of external entity, we miss the point. It is also precisely why we fail. The fact is, the way to a better relationship with that which we call time, is through self-discipline, habits, grit, conscientiousness, a forging ahead; honouring the preciousness that is us, our desires and dreams to attain some good through the application of skill and effort.

It would follow then that if time is us, and time is life, what we would attain in life depends on how we treat ourselves, our dreams, our ambitions, for as said elsewhere, we do not waste time, it is ourselves we waste, when we do procrastinate.

During my research for this work, I came across many situations that made me begin to question our relationship with time. Most of us have become slaves to time. We have time all around us more than ever before, (time-telling devices that is), and yet even more than ever, we fret about time. We have more gadgets to prompt and remind us of the preciousness of time and how much of it is apparently available to us at any moment, and yet for most of us, these reminders only remain a source of stress. No wonder our relationship with time tends to be love-hate at best. The question begs to be asked: Is being "busy" supposed to be indicative of productivity? In a lot of ways, this is what appears to be the mind-set.

There is joy in simple things. Just look around you. If we pay attention, it would be clear enough. Life is meant to be simple; but everywhere, we insist on making a complexity of it. That is the tragedy of our modern existence. Taking that which we call time for example, we have made a fetish of it. Time seems to rule humanity instead of humanity mastering time. In much of western culture, we have made time into a linear, irrecoverable entity, forever vanishing. But, "what is he rambling about?" you might be asking. I have a couple of questions for you: Is time precious? You bet it is. Is time limited? That depends on one's perspective.

You may or may not agree with me. But I don't believe time properly understood, is a linear, limited concept. Time is abundant, ever-present, evolving and renewing.

Time is everything, and yet time is nothing. Time is what it is that each makes it to be. The true value of time relates to what each of us has to show for it, our work, our achievements, our investment in others, and our personal legacy for having passed by this earth.

Time is personal, but also communal. By communal, I mean, every society has its own unique concept of and relationship with time. We shall discuss this further elsewhere. Likewise, time is universal; but also local, and particular. It is at once simple and complex. Time is the servant, but also the master of life. It is the governor and the governed; it manages us even as we seek to manage it.

Time may even be the deceit that tomorrow is yours; that you have forever to accomplish your dreams, and yet, as anyone who has ever failed can attest, time is the hope that tomorrow will come, and with it, another chance, one more opportunity for a shot at whatever great or humble enterprise calls forth one's energies.

We have said elsewhere, that time is among other things, linear. Indeed, time as a linear concept is not universal. It is especially particular to western culture. Within this construct, time flows unidirectionally along a defined path in discrete chunks, which pass us by irrecoverably. What a recipe for panic! Is it any wonder that time seems to be such a great source of stress for many?

Time as individually determined, but also a socio-cultural construct

It is arguable that linear time is a social construct, designed for the control of production in the capitalist enterprise. Let's take a typical worker and the working day. Production time is usually "9-5". Time for this fellow starts at 9 in the ante meridian, and ends at 5 in the prime meridian. It is in this time slot that the fellow must justify his or her wages. It is where the focus is for all productive purposes.

The focus in relation to time is work. But why must it be so? Isn't life much more than work? In the linear construct of time, therefore, our relationship with time appears to be not just simple, but simplistic. There is an important difference here, dear reader I am sure you appreciate that.

We have said that time is both simple and complex. Unfortunately, in relation to time, there are many simple things that we seem to have rendered unnecessarily complex. Take for example, the important act of awakening from sleep. It used to be that as a necessary function of life, people slept and awoke when they felt refreshed enough for the day's task ahead. Their bodies alerted them. Of course, before organic farming became a commercial fashion, the neighbourhood rooster would crow at dawn to remind all that a new day had broken; another opportunity, a chance to make a difference, to seek, to find, to work a little, play a little, to give a little of the self, to receive, to thrive. Enough unto the day that is, was always just that, ENOUGH. Time was ours to use, however it suited us. Hardly any rush was called for. Everything got done in its own time. And yes, it all got done. Simple. Right?

May be, but not anymore. Now we invest in Apps that forcibly "eject" us from our sleeping haven into a harsh daybreak, eyes bleary and bodies achy and protesting. Time has become a slave master, the human, the slave-servant. How good is that? I don't know how anyone can be happy with this kind of existence. Yes, I said "existence", for this is not life. It cannot be, yet how we do persist with the status quo. Why?

Consider sleep, time and productivity and what they really mean in the larger scheme of life. We skip, skim on and even seek to abandon and trade sleep for what we think is "more time" for productivity, and yet research after research shows that quality sleep is the bedrock of robust health, mental alertness and focus, and ultimately productivity. We live a life of survival and our default time setting seems to read, "Survival mode", because we have managed to engineer our human selves to become but mere economic factors.

To be happy, it is not enough to survive; we must thrive, and relentlessly so. It is a demand from the self, and our duty to meet that demand. What do you mean to time…a mere productive unit? How does that feel? Not very nice I would presume. Where is the respect in being a MERE economic unit?

If being a "mere productive unit" doesn't sit well with you, what are you going to do about it? The starting point is, what does time mean to you? Shall we hear your answer?

If you are concerned, it's up to you to take action. Un-time yourself. What do I mean by that? Well, isn't it time to put time in its proper place in your life? You bet it is! Come along. You will be amazed at how much you stand to gain, and achieve in terms of your own personal productivity when you de-couple from the tyranny of time.

That time is valuable, is beyond question. Like any valuable commodity, there have been many attempts at extracting more value from whatever time there may be at hand in any given situation. This is totally rational and is to be expected. To this end, there have been various attempts regarding how for example, to "compress" years into weeks, the work-week into hours, and days into minutes. In effect how to get more out of less time. Desperate times indeed! But do we all approach time in the same way? How about a notion, that your time may be more unique than you know. This is the subject we consider next.

Of Personal Individual Time:

What is individual time? In *Time Warped*, Claudia Hammond, argues that our individual, personal perception of time varies depending on various factors, some of which are in our sphere of control and others not. That means your concept of time and mine are not and cannot be the same. Why? It's simple. The circumstances of your birth are not the same as mine. Your family, social, and psychological influences among many others are not the same as the next fellow, not even those of your siblings. Even twins do not share the exact same time–date stamp of birth.

So now, you see why our concepts and perceptions of time may be different? What's more, these individual perceptions of time may vary from day-to-day, and even event-to-event. One day, time may seem to drag on especially when one is bored. On the contrary, it may appear to pass rather quickly when we are engaged in a joyous event for example. Of course, this is something you and I can both relate to.

However, Claudia Hammond argues, that despite what we may think, it is not the "flow" of time that varies, but our personal perception of this "flow" as influenced by our particular circumstances. Factors such as our emotional state, and our memory can be especially important in this state of affairs. It is also instructive when we consider that our emotions and body temperature can actually affect our perception of time. This is the position of the psychologist Hudson Hoag who has done extensive work in this area.

Regarding emotions, it is argued that the more strongly emotionally aroused a person is, the more slowly time may appear to pass. I remember once, long ago, getting stuck in a public lift or elevator as other users of the language call it. The 5 minutes we had to wait for the response team seemed like an eternity. I kid you not! But I can assure you, to the rescuers, they were there at our side in record time, seconds, it might have seemed. So, you see, 5 minutes can seem differently to different folks, depending on their particular circumstances. Of course, when one is stuck in a lift with 6 others, and the mirror has begun to appear misty from exhaled breath and psychological and physical perspiration, one can hardly be convinced that 5 minutes is anything less than an eternity. I sincerely wish no one ever, has to endure such hellish wait ever. But of course, that was my perception influenced by personal fear and all the negative thoughts that must have been racing through my mind at the speed of light. Hahaha! Yes, I can laugh now. But it was no laughing matter then. I am sure you may have recollections of your own.

But given the passage of the years, I cannot really tell you the amount of time we had to wait for rescue. I cringe recalling this, so to my memory, perhaps it was more than an eternity of wait. If it had been a positive experience, I would perhaps remember the time as having passed rather swiftly. In either scenario, time was relative to my personal prevailing factors including the emotional, mental, psychological, and the physical.

So, what are we saying? That Time is what you make it? Perhaps. But more importantly, it is what your personal state "dictates". According to the writer and researcher, Siffre, our personal internal time is governed by external stimuli. However, we may have little control over certain external stimuli, such as the weather, as to whether it is hot or cold, Winter or Summer or the warmth of a Spring Day.

Another writer, Amelia Hunt, however, urges us to "create" more time for all our work by slowing down time. She argues that the more attention we pay to something, the more slowly time appears to flow. I am sure we are all familiar with being late for a function and having to wait for the train or bus. That focus on the arrival of the next train or bus makes the arrival seem forever long. Do you recall your own experience? I am sure you can relate. The opposite of this is the effect of routine. Generally, routine is said to "shorten "time. But then why are these important?

Claudia Hammond emphasises that "time dictates the pattern of our lives: when we work, when we eat, even when we choose to celebrate". We have said time is "us", and we are time; that time is, because we are. It is a strange connection, but true. In a nutshell, we do influence time as much as time influences us.

But what about social conditioning, as it relates to attitudes towards time? We do not live in a vacuum. Many of our personal habits are gleaned from our particular environments. These may be social, cultural, and even the economic and psychological make-up of our surroundings. In this sense, our individual perception of time can also be socially determined. This is the subject of our next discussion.

Time as Socially Determined

The concept of "punctuality" is, I dare say, a child of the industrial revolution; a "western" construct meant to serve business and economic ends. It is based on the notion that "time is money". But is that all? Is this all there is to time? Is money all time can yield? Is money everything? Think about it.

Don't get me wrong. Punctuality is crucial for collaboration, for social coordination and all. We all know how utterly annoying it can be to have to wait on one or more people to show up in order to get a particular activity started. So, yes, punctuality is vital. But it still remains in its present deployment and understanding, a transactional construct. There is nothing wrong with that. But there is more to time than mere "punctuality", keeping us all synchronized as it were. –Industrial line style. I trust you do get the point. How does it feel to be strung along with others, day in, day out? –A number, perhaps. An economic unit; a number to yield other numbers; cash, dividends, capital gains, stocks up; stocks sideways, and what have you.

The "almost-everything-is- time" relationship we tend to have with this entity is hardly productive in any proper, real sense. If we desire to be truly productive, we must choose the optimal over the maximal, now and always. Optimal is a win-win where-as maximal is invariably a win-lose. Optimal yields balance, a maximal mentality only affords a seemingly full yield in one quarter and, a depletion in the other.

We can see this play out in many arenas of our lives. When people talk of achieving work-life balance, what they really mean is optimal productivity and living. That is, the optimization of productive outcomes without sacrificing personal wellbeing.

Rush, rush, rush achieves little by itself. It is also a relatively recent behaviour as explained elsewhere. Many traditional societies of old, (Please note the emphasis on "traditional") in the eastern and other parts of the world including Africa, Asia and Native America have customarily had a more "expansive" concept of time. In these cultures, Time embodies less an emphasis on punctuality and more an attention to celebration. For instance, if invited to dinner at say 6pm, that time is only a guide to say that dinner is in the evening after your work is done. Well, how problematic, won't you say? Yes and No.

In this context, dinner starts when the guests arrive, when all is ready, when we are ready. Annoying for the western-raised fellow whose 6 pm is just that, 6pm. Life is easier that way. I agree. But in these societies, the dinner itself is not important. It is all about the celebration. Once you understand this basic concept, you begin to appreciate the situation.

Why is the dinner itself secondary? Let's face it, as one African writer so eloquently put it, when you invite people to dinner and they accept, *it is not because they themselves have no food in their homes*; it is only because they care and want to celebrate your good fortune, hospitality and kindness and in the process, help cure your otherwise loneliness with your wealth. So, you see, it is all about the celebration. Dinner can go hang, (so to speak). That African writer was Chinua Achebe, writing in the Classic, ***Things Fall Apart.***

You get the point I presume. So next time you find yourself in a society that treats time differently, remember, there may be far more fundamental considerations with social values and norms at play. I bet you will be better served just going with the "flow". In other words, "un-time" yourself; stay present; enjoy what is; celebrate the moment.

Time pressure is arguably one of the very worst stresses of our time. You would realize that in societies such as the one described above, just as in your world too, things invariably do get done, in spite of what might seem to the outsider as a wanton waste of time. The difference is in the emphasis as to what is primary. In these societies, time is a mere tool, not a master dictator of how things must be. –They the people, the society have chosen to master time. They are intentional in their dealings with time. Do you think the host and the early arrivals do not know what time it is they were supposed to be having dinner? Of course, they do. That they tolerate and embrace the delay is testament to what they consider as important in the moment. – A feast of friendship, relaxation and socio-cultural renewal; an affirmation of that which is of utmost value in life- the cultivation and nurturing of relationships. Time in this equation is only a low-key factor, a facilitator.

Of Time in small packages: The Four Seasons.

The ultimate measure of freedom is the ability to control one's time. Let's face it your most important time is that which you control. That is what is truly yours. What are you doing with your ultimate resource, that portion of time, which is truly yours? That is the subject of this chapter.

It has been said that the world is an illusion. Therefore, maybe trying to do the apparently logical is not always in our best interest. It has also been suggested that maybe we can make better progress by learning to cooperate with the world around us; going with the flow; giving up resistance. What are your thoughts? Counter intuitive, you think? Maybe! But no matter our individual thoughts and ideas, the fact remains that nature has its own very peculiar rhythm of time. Thus, there are, the well-known four seasons: Winter, Spring, Summer and Autumn or Fall, if you live across the pond. In some jurisdictions, there are the Wet and Dry seasons. Some have the Monsoon season and a host of others in-between. It is all a matter of geography. We do not get to choose the seasons in our weather charts. But whatever they may be, the seasons are there for a reason. They do a brilliant job of illustrating how we may live and use our time. If we need inspiration with dealing with time, let's look to nature. Time is many things to many people. What you may think it is, may not be by some other measure. If you are used to Winter, Spring, Summer and Fall, you may think that is time as nature has planned it. But as you may be aware by now, you will be wrong. That is your illusion. Your geography has set you up to think in absolute terms. There are other realities of time. All are valid for those who are governed by whatever time may be, wherever that is. Always remember that. There are always others too, with their realty as valid as yours.

Time is relative. That is a proven fact. It is also true that apart from the speed of light, the truth of every other thing in life depends on one's frame of reference. Perspective is therefore key. It can help us reframe a tragedy, or a bad experience so we get a positive vibe, a feeling, an awakening from it to energize us and do great things going forward. But it can also fool us when we think we are right and the other is wrong. We become rigid, unyielding and unreasonable. In short, our perspective can steal our reason from us, and with that our ability to grow, learn, be better human beings and to find greater peace.

In his book, ***A Brief History of Time***, Professor Stephen Hawkings tells us that time is relative. He explains that even-though this relativity is hardly noticeable; it does have significant impacts on our everyday life and activities. Think about it. Apparently, your time and my time are not the same. Time depends on where you and I are in relation to each other. Our personal time even dictates how age shows on us, even if we are twins. He explains for example, that a twin whose abode is on a mountaintop will age marginally faster than his sibling living at sea level.

Albert Einstein gifted us the theory of relativity and the realisation that time is relative and is unique to the perspective of the observer. Our perception of time is usually as moving forward, from past to present to future. We also measure time through its tendency to engender increased entropy. – A movement from a healthy organised state to "chaos". Do you begin to see why time as you know and embrace it is an illusion?

Of Consistency, Perspective and more.

In work by Philip Zimbardo and John Boyd, they suggest that we can live a better life by discovering our relationship with time.

Steve Jobs is reputed to have once stated near the end of his dear life, "It's clear that the most precious resource we all have is time". You bet the man knew what he was talking about. He was a man of vision and action. He knew the value of time beyond mere rhetoric. Time was his friend for its enablement of his creative pursuits and technological achievements. In the end, time too was the foe that robbed us of him and his further participation in that which we call life and we are only left with what else might have been, had he only lived a little longer. Sad, yes; but true. Time, is indeed the precious resource; the ultimate gift we have in this life. We had better see it as such, treat it as such, but most of all, use and value it as such. It is the only way to stave off regret.

Life, with anything else connected to it demands that if we desire to get the most of it, we must resolve to do those routine, even boring little but important things that make it valuable. This is the magic of consistency.

As the public speaker, Simon Sinek once explained regarding the importance of consistency, we achieve results not through one time application of effort, however mighty that effort might be, but by the everyday consistent application of small bits of efforts, like brushing one's teeth each day, exercising a bit each morning. By themselves, these everyday acts, may not seem much, nor yield much, but with consistency of application, over time, their effects do and will add up, in stronger teeth and healthy bodies. So, it must be for us regarding our relationship with time, if we desire to make it work for us, we must consistently honour time as our most precious resource.

For most of us, our relationship with time is a complex mix of love-hate. We love time when it affords us our little distractions, but hate it when it compels us to re-examine our priorities as in the face of life circumstances, when time may seem to be against us. But time also influences each of us differently as we have learnt elsewhere and from Professor Hawkings' narrative regarding the relativity of individual time.

Now, what does it matter what you or my time perspective is? It does matter because how we view events in time has a big impact on our behaviour, and how we live our lives, and therefore, our happiness or unhappiness. When you think about the fact that in all our struggles through life, the bottom line is our search for individual happiness, this counts for a lot indeed. For example, an attitude of gratitude can transform a past–negative experience into a past-positive one. In other words, perception is everything, and it may be more important to our present state of happiness than the reality of things past. It's important to remember this.

Now, consider this: Experts argue that in any situation, there are choices to be made regarding the off-taking of rewards. For example, while the present-hedonist, the pleasure-driven fellow who only cares about instant pleasure is obsessed with deriving maximal pleasure, and the present-fatalist, the fellow for whom all is dark and nothing good can be found in present existence, has given up hope to the dictates of the gods that be, the future-minded individual cultivates the strength of hope to see a better tomorrow than today and so to plod on, inch by inch by ever-achieving effort until the goal has been attained.

But then again, why is this important in the context of time? It is because time controls us; every aspect of our being, attainments and yes, even our emotions. The expression: "give it time…" is not without merit. Future-fatalism, the irrational fear of what could go wrong tomorrow, does lead to anxiety; present-orientation on the other hand, can confer restful peace. The events remain the same, but the time perspective makes all the difference between a feeling of anxiety and that of restful peace. It is all about perspective, and our perspective governs our very relationship with Time.

Therefore, as we are beginning to see, reaping the rewards of time is not by chance, it necessarily demands deliberate planning and execution for its attainment. Ironically, successful future–orientation requires present stability for proper execution. What this means is that one cannot be hopeful for a better future without an appreciation of the gifts of the present. It has a name. It is called *Gratitude* for what is. The trick is to reach for a healthy balance. How do you do that? Count your blessings; acknowledge how far you have come by getting to know yourself first and your journey to-date. With that solid base of appreciation, you are in a better position to begin to take the necessary steps to make the best use of the time available to you to further your goals. Self-acknowledgement and self-knowledge through appropriate and unfiltered introspection is the starting point to "healing" our relationship with Time. Let this work for you. It matters that we manage this relationship appropriately for our greater benefit.

Time and productivity.

Growing up, we were told to manage our time wisely if we wanted to get things done, be productive and get ahead in life. Good advice it was and still is. "Time management" is still a great catchphrase in corporate circles. However, time is not all there is to productivity, and neither is productivity all about time. Recent research shows that perhaps, more than time, and managing time per se, we would be better served if we paid attention to managing our energy levels throughout the day in relation to what tasks need to be accomplished.

In other words, if we want to accomplish more, our task is not to manage time; our duty is to manage ourselves, and critically, our various resources. The reality is that as we get older, time becomes even more important, both for its scarcity, because we know we are running out of it with our ever-incremental approach to whatever our individual "finish line" is, and its abundance, because we tend to have it on our hands, say due to retirement, and have to figure out how to spend it. Yet, if we want to accomplish more, our task is not to manage time. Though it may seem counterintuitive, our duty is to manage ourselves, and critically, our various energies. As a crude analogy, do you recall a time of illness? You had plenty of time and perhaps would have loved to get back to that task that needed finishing, but were you able to? I believe we both know the answer to that. There are things that are more important to our productivity than the mere factor of time. Indeed, of what use is time if our personal energies are inadequate to use the time we have to accomplish our objectives?

During my research for this book, I came across a brilliant piece of work by Jim Loehr and Tony Schwartz, "The Power of Full Engagement". It caught my attention because of my own personal battles with time and energy levels at the time. The authors' argument is essentially that to be able to perform our tasks effectively, we need to relentlessly cultivate and manage our human energies and capacities in all aspects of life. But what is the practical application of this, you might ask? Well, take your physical self, and your energy for example. Without adequate rest to recharge, you will become grumpy and lethargic. Therefore, to remain sharp and bright during the day, you require a good night's rest.

Have you ever wondered why some people sometimes seem to be on edge, ready to attack over very minor incidents? It is likely because they have an emotional deficit. They have a deficit balance in their personal emotional bank account. When we are emotionally depleted, we tend to be more likely to act irrationally than at other times. How do you balance that account? Feed your emotions; do things that make you feel alive, happy, cheerful, energized and which are safe, sound and beneficial for your long-term wellbeing.

There is also our mental self which needs looking after, making sure it is energized, in tip-top form and primed to serve us. How effective were you the last time you had "things on your mind" and were trying to get some work done? Probably not very effective, you would no doubt admit. When you are worried, life becomes miserable both for yourself and those around you. The other types of energy we need to both harness and manage are the psychological, but also the spiritual (for those who can relate). How do we harness such energies? We shall deal with that separately in greater detail later.

However, whether we believe it or not, there is evidence, both empirical and anecdotal, to the effect that people who hold an anchor (based on whatever belief or non-belief system they may have) outside of themselves to deal with life's challenges are far more able to cope with fundamental challenges, hardships and sudden personal trials than those who do not. Call this anchor a spiritual or psychological essence. It makes no difference.

However, like any resource available to us, we will have greater and better use of these human energies only if we deliberately and continually replenish and nourish, as well as make careful and intelligent use of them. In short Loehr and Schwartz suggest that if one wants to be able to fully engage with life, one must learn to manage one's energies.

So, there you have it. Be intentional if you want to be productive, stop fretting about time. You cannot control time, but you can manage yourself and your energies and therefore how you relate to and engage with Time, and use that essence to your ultimate advantage. But what does being intentional mean? For starters you would need to have a clear knowledge base about your relationship with time. This is the subject of our next discussion.

Time Management: An Assessment Exercise.

In responding to the statements below, fill in each blank with the number from the rating scale that indicates the frequency with which you do each activity. Assess your behaviour as it is, not as you would like it to be. Bear in mind that the usefulness of this instrument depends on your ability to accurately assess your own behaviour.

Rating Scale:

0= Never 1= Seldom 2= Sometimes 3= Often 4= Always

_____ 1. I start my day with a plan.

_____ 2. I keep "an orderly" work environment.

_____ 3. I avoid the temptation of multi-tasking and focus on one task at a time.

_____ 4. I focus on doing my most important and high-reward task first.

_____ 5. I know what my most productive period is during the day and make sure to protect it for productive work.

_____ 6. I do not feel guilty saying "no" to interruptions during my day.

_____ 7. I pay attention to and am aware of potential time-wasting scenarios, and take action accordingly.

_____ 8. I plan my time use and stick to it.

_____ 9. I use "captive time" such as a wait for the train to do something productive.

_____ 10. I plan my day and try to do similar un-important non-urgent tasks such as answering emails; returning phone calls at a go during the day.

_____ 11. I make an effort to have results to account for time spent each day.

_____ 12. I plan for some personal time during the day to enjoy my own company and reflect.

_____ 13. I regularly set aside thinking time to consider things going on in my life.

_____ 14. I usually set clearly defined long-term objectives and work towards them.

_____ 15. I continually try to find ways to use my time more efficiently.

How did it go? Now that you have some idea as to what your relationship with time might be it is time to take action for the better. All that is required is for you to do more of the good stuff, you know, those habits that serve your better interest, and to do less of the other things that work against your productivity.

You know yourself better than anyone else. The exercise is meant as a guide, a wake-up call, and to motivate you to do better. I trust that is how you view it too. If so, we have succeeded. Great! Talking about you knowing yourself, and how this relates to time and productivity is the basis of our next chapter.

"Time is the supreme gift. It is all that matters; nothing else matters a damn thing, except life itself. Yet, our warped perception of time usually means we fail to appreciate our today, and miss our present, because we are often too pre-occupied with tomorrow and lost in a future not given."-NB-D.

Chapter Three

Leveraging for Productivity.

"Your time on this earth is limited", Steve Jobs once reminded us (We discussed this earlier). That means if you desire amazing productivity, you will need to tap into something more fundamental to abundant achievement than the deployment of raw talent and time. You need a little booster to lift you up and to get you up there. Just like a space shuttle does. Being up there can be tough, but managing to get up there is an even greater feat. That is why space shuttles have rocket boosters. The rocket does not replace the shuttle's abilities, but it does give it unstoppable momentum. Now this is a crude over-simplification of course and a very rough analogy to our cause, but I trust you are in on the import.

The rocket is the leverage that the shuttle needs to get ahead on its mission to overcome the natural downward pull of gravity. Your endeavour is no different. There are many forces that will conspire to pull you down back to base. Some will be your own fault; others will be out of your control. But it does not make any difference. If you fail, no one will congratulate you on your failure. Success is the only measure that counts. With a little leverage, however, you may be able to overcome the odds and pull away to success. It all starts with you. What is your leverage?

The Power of Leverage:

There are two options when it comes to productivity: The "normal" obvious and slow way, and the leveraged, fast and enhanced way. The "normal" way is also invariably, the harder of the two. The smart way relies on the power of leverage, a little help from the utilisation of tools and other resources beyond the "hard way" of doing things.

By leverage, what is meant is the ability to use whatever quality or advantage we may possess, such as our minds, creativity, skills; other resources whether material, physical or fiscal; specialist knowledge; even machinery and our ability to influence and lead other people to gain our desired effect or result. Here are some examples of leverage in history.

Leverage through the ages:

The Stone Age: This so-called pre-historic period was characterised by human use of "primitive" stone tools. Today we have the luxury of calling these implements "primitive" but at the time, they were a real cutting-edge technology. Before these implements were invented, there was nothing like them. It is estimated that the Stone Age lasted at least 2.5 million years. The Stone Age was only supplanted when humans discovered the use of metal and started making tools and weapons with bronze, thus ushering in the Bronze Age.

The Bronze Age: As you can determine, bronze is generally more adaptable to more uses than stone. It therefore represents progress, and by leveraging the use of metal in place of stone, humans were able to do more, and achieve more in less time, with less effort and resources. Stone was appropriate for its age, and so was bronze. Time moved on and so did human civilization and the peculiar requirements for greater wealth creation. Welcome to the Iron Age.

The Iron Age: The Iron Age is said to be the period that generally followed the Stone and Bronze Ages. During this period, many civilizations in Africa, Europe and Asia began making implements, common tools and weapons from iron and steel. Now, it isn't that iron is superior to bronze. In fact, iron was seen in the bronze era as an inferior material because weapons fashioned with iron were deemed as not being as strong or durable as those made of bronze. It was only later when the knowledge of steel production became common, that iron came into its own and gained currency over bronze in the manufacture of weapons and implements. Steel is of course a much harder metal, and is made through a process involving heating iron with carbon.

Steel therefore offered better leverage with weapons, and naturally, it took over as the material of choice in industry. But during these periods under review, weapons and working tools were largely fashioned using hard human labour. In everything part of the process was human-labour intensive from beating poles and sheets of metal to heating the same and bending them into desirable shape. Everything was a matter of pure sweat. Enter the industrial revolution next and things were getting better for the productive endeavour.

The Industrial Age: The Industrial Age describes the processes of change and transition to new and more efficient methods of manufacturing and enterprise, changing from the more labour-intensive agrarian and handicraft economy to one underpinned by the use of power-driven tools and machinery. It is argued that this so-called industrial revolution occurred as a result of the desire of agro-based societies to become more urbanized and industrialized.

In the 18th Century when the Scottish author, philosopher and political economist, Adam Smith, was writing his classic: ***An Enquiry into the Nature and Causes of the Wealth of Nations,*** wealth originated from the soil, that is, from nature by way of agrarian pursuits. In the expansive period of the Industrial Age which began with the so-called industrial revolution in Great Britain, and later elsewhere in the second half of the 18th Century, (said to be around 1760), hand-powered tools were largely replaced by power-driven machinery. Thus, hand looms were increasingly replaced by power looms and the steam engine held sway in critical ways.

Further down the centuries, we have continued to witness the evolution of the labour enterprise in the utilisation of the evident power of leverage to create dramatic increases in output, wealth and general welfare around and across the globe. Machines are now giving humans even more leverage power than before. So, as you can see, it is all progress in motion from age to age.

We are currently in the so-called Digital Age. It is arguably the most advanced of the development Ages in human history. It is the age of knowledge and information where your name is money and your shopping habits can be mined to make riches. How are you positioning yourself in this revolution in wealth creation? The amazing thing is that unlike stone or steel or agro-products, anyone can create knowledge, monetise it and become wealthy, even beyond his or her wildest dreams. However, it takes knowing "how". That "how", is through the application of thought. Goethe was right. He said it long ago:

There is no problem so hard that it cannot be solved by the diligent application of thought.

I believe he was talking to us today. Your thoughts are completely yours to think. Use them for wealth creation and to develop strategies for a better life.

Leveraging in The Digital Age:

We have noted elsewhere that nobody succeeds alone. That is true. But to be even widely successful, that is where the power of leverage comes into its own. I once had a client. His problem could be framed as: *Why was he so hardworking but had nothing to show for it?* Indeed, he was HARD-WORKING. You see he was a tutor, and a very good one at that. I know this because his students loved him and he helped them get good grades. But it turned out that he could only fit in about 5 appointments per day because he went round the homes of his students to tutor. He was always tired from all the commuting and the teaching. To him, his tiredness and the fact that his students got good results were marks of his hard work and a justification for better returns. Of course, he had options: He could have invested in skills for a better-paying job of his fancy, but nothing is guaranteed and he may well have found that he would have had to join the job-seeker queue after his studies. He actually felt that being a mortgage broker might be an option for him. Mind you, this was going to be a totally new field for him.

But he really loved his work as a tutor. We considered having his students congregate at a central location such as a hired classroom in a suitably located school. That way, it's the students who would have to commute variously while he of course saved himself the commute to their various homes. This of course was not workable because parents wanted their wards at home after school, and to see them getting extra help with their studies.

We worked out finally, that he could consider using any of the many apps, like Skype or Zoom to deliver his lessons. He was resistant to the idea at first. But guess what, when he mooted the idea to his students, not only did his existing ones jump at the opportunity, but also when they told their friends, many of them enrolled too. In his own words, "How cool is that!" The covid-19 situation has of course made online tuition commonplace but this was before the practice exploded.

His income shot up; his days of commuting were over immediately; he was no longer the tired whining fellow of the past. This is the power of leverage. Break old patterns. Think better ways of achieving your end goals. Free yourself and your time for other things in life. Leverage is the golden alchemy of the modern time.

Leveraging as the modern wealth genie:

This is a fact. Today leverage creates wealth in exponential quantities. We count fiscal wealth in the billions and trillions. Material wealth has exploded. It is said that your average mobile phone that you carry about in the palm of your hand is more powerful than the computing systems that first helped launch mankind to the moon and back in the later part of the1960s. Imagine what that computer system cost at the time. How much did you pay for yours? I know what I paid for mine. Now that's value. Leverage creates incredible value as you can see. Today the real source of wealth, is no longer nature or machine power, it is data and knowledge. Your mind, your creative mind that is, is a gold mine, a diamond mine, and all the mines of all the precious metals you can think of combined, and more. Businesses such as the Googles and Amazons and the Facebooks of our time have attested to this. Facebook is free for you and I to use; so is Google. Yet these companies control quantities of wealth that far out-strip the Gross Domestic Products (GDPs) of many nations on earth.

These companies have also made countless individuals incredibly wealthy beyond any means achievable by way of the Agrarian or Industrial Age path of wealth creation. It is what continued development and utilisation of the power of leverage can do for anyone who pays heed. As a collective, we have never been wealthier; never had it so good. That there are stark pockets of dire poverty still in many places in our midst is not an issue of the lack of wealth and plenty but one of distribution and the politics thereof, one could argue.

The good news however, is that there is the potential for wealth available to everyone. Why? It is because we all have a self, and that is our most valuable resource for wealth-creation. Leverage is what makes it possible for successful people, ordinary humans often with no greater fundamental special skills or advantage over your average Joe Male or Joan Female to achieve incredible results with whatever cards nature has dealt them. Think about it. The difference is that they have learnt to harness the incredible superior energy of the supreme enabler, The Power of Leverage, to their ultimate advantage.

Do you remember our tutor friend? The fact is that our friend was initially engaged in a linear productivity relationship involving his HARDWORK, time, and skills and his results showed this accordingly. There is only so much one a can achieve in a day using the facility of the sole self. He was only able to tutor 5 students as a maximum per day. With the intervention of the leverage of technology however, he was able to easily tutor multiples of that, and the icing on the cake…tiredness was no longer an issue. That is the power of leverage. The leverage of technology accelerated his results and success. But what does this mean to you in the context of "Why time management is a waste of your time and what your options are"?

You are called to embrace change, to evolve, to grow. You are urged to not get comfortable with the way things are and how you have "always done them". It is a call to learn, to seek out new ways of being and doing; to be inquisitive, to think and see with eyes and to dream of a better future; to crave new and fresh insights, for the world is evolving and what worked yesterday, may with a little boost work even better today. By all means enjoy what is, but do not settle for what has been.

Progress calls forth. I do hope it is clear by now, that there is only so much you or I can do given the time we have per day to attain the kind of success and results we most desire and are indeed capable of. Hard work may have been good enough some time ago, but not anymore. Now, to succeed more, you and I need the Power of Leverage to do the heavy lifting for us, so to speak. As our tutor in the story quickly found out, the market rewards value, and not mere fatiguing hard work.

Ask yourself, what are you delivering to the market with your skill and know-how in the form of products and services? More importantly, what tools are you using to grow that delivery to the market place? Leverage makes all the difference. But what does this mean to you and I?

Let's play a game. Why don't you take a sheet of paper, get a pen and try the following?

Exercise: My Personal leverage tools.

Let's answer this question: What tools of leverage are you using to grow your delivery to the market place? Take your time. Be honest. Think hard and write down everything.

What were your results? Any insights? Is there anything in particular that stood out, anything that spoke to you? How have you been short-changing yourself and your dreams? Leverage is everything. Don't be so hard on yourself; learn to master the art and science of good-old leverage and it will serve you well indeed. Let's see what your fortunes could look like if you dared enough. Read on.

Leveraging and the self:

How do you leverage yourself? Know that knowledge is the new gold. Things have moved on from the natural resource–led economy to the knowledge–driven wealth creation enterprise. Your mind is the new gold mine. Think deeply and you may just unearth magical gold. But first, you have to cultivate the mine, which is the mind, grow its potential to think creative solutions and in time, with practice and dedication, it will start yielding value without compare.

You begin by investing in yourself. You do so through self–improvement; working on yourself to become incrementally better each day. You work to improve your skills such as communication, negotiations, empathy, decision-making, leadership and general people management know-how. You do so by building better habits and superior work ethics and by making self-care a priority through taking care of you, for without you, nothing is. The more valuable you are as an invested option, the better the ROI. No. I am not talking here of return on investment, though that may be a valid outcome, I am talking of RETURN ON INTENTION. You must be intentional in investing in yourself, and you are sure to reap the rewards. In short, as far as wealth creation and productivity go, **you are your very best option,** for you can only multiply that which you have to leverage. The better you are as an investable entity, the more attractive you will be to the market and the greater the reward you stand to gain. When you become more valuable to the market place, a unit of your time will command more value and you will be compensated correspondingly. Your productivity measured by the common "monetary outcome" will explode not because of long hours and "sweat and toil", but because of the leverage of your more valuable self. Your result in this case has very little to do with time management and all to do with your choosing the option of leverage of a more invested and valuable self. Think about it.

So, here you have it. You have a choice: To continue with the illusion of time "management" and keep managing your 1440 units per day, trading those and minimal skills linearly in the hope of a reward, or to embrace progressive change and hitch the resources of your mind and talents to leverage. Try it. It will put power in your sails.

Therefore, if you desire great success, learn to embrace change. The change is the reality that knowledge is supreme in our current dispensation. Things have shifted. What you knew as a sure thing yesterday may be passé, today. Life is itself a series of transitions, after transition. The secret is to learn to manage these transitions. Keep abreast of the times and put leverage to work for you.

Talking of leverage, how about if you could conjure time; wave the proverbial magic wand and presto! You had more time to play and work with? How utterly fantastical would that be! Most of us bemoan the dearth of enough hours in the day to get all our work done. Well, there is good and bad news. The bad news is that this only means we are working less than efficiently; that we are making less than efficient use of our time. The good news however, you would be glad to know, is that we can "make" more time out of our nature-given 24-hour day to get that which needs doing done. Hahaha! How magical is that! Fantastic, won't you say? Yep! But this has nothing to do with incantations or whatever we believe magic entails.

Indeed, the very best of magic, from David Copperfield's the vanishing of the Statue of Liberty live act to the transmutation of paper into pigeons is all about clever tricks. The same applies to making more time. It is about doing what is important first before any other. This is the subject of our next topic.

The Art of Prioritization

Knowing what comes first, what is of essence and acting accordingly is the Art of Prioritization. It works every time. Long ago, I read a book on time management. What has stuck with me till this day is the single line: Go hunt elephants, not ants. The metaphor is meant to represent approaches to tackling significant, and less significant tasks respectively.

Your elephants are the most important tasks that will make a significant difference once you do them. Your elephants are indeed those meaningful tasks, big or small that underlie your productivity and success. You must actively seek these and work on them. It is one way of being intentional with the use of your time. Seek out your elephants and feed them. Feed them with passion and attention and they will reward you. In other words, focus on those few significant tasks that will yield you the biggest returns on your time and effort. It sounds simple. It is not. It is not easy to master, but it can be mastered and it yields unparalleled value, indeed. Try it.

As we have noted it goes without saying, that if we are to be productive with our use of time, we need to refocus and be intentional regarding our most significant tasks, and how we deploy the most important resources of ours accordingly. Time is arguably second only to health in life. With time and good health, everything else that is humanly possible, can be attained. We next explore the relationship between self-management and *Time*.

Chapter Four

"Wo/man, Know thyself ". – Socrates

Self-Management and Time: What Relationship?

We have been discussing leverages of various kinds and how they relate to personal productivity. We will now consider the leverage of time. Yes, Time is itself a lever. In fact, it is one of the greatest, together with good health, and know-how. Our success is impacted by how we leverage the time we have and that is determined by our context. We are used to framing time and its management through a context of scarcity and limitation. We say time is limited; time is running out; time waits for no wo/man. But what if we shifted our perspective, and expanded our context to include time as a friend? What if we developed a relationship with time such that it was no longer the "enemy" of productivity and success, but a co-creator, a friend, a "business" partner? What would change?

I would argue that the difficulty with *Time* is not the managing; nor is it the disciplining of the self in relation to the management of time itself. The greater task lies in the management of the management of the self so as to achieve a more purposeful utility of time. In other words, to be able to have greater leverage with time, there is a relationship that is called for between ourselves on the one hand, and the resource called *Time* on the other. This has been the basis of our discussion and is the premise of this book, that to achieve greater productivity, it is more important to strive to achieve better management of the self, relative to time rather than trying to manage time itself. Crucially however, it is learning how to manage our "self-management" that is the key to results. How do we achieve this? Let's explore further.

Managing for Self-Management

Most of us are familiar with time management, and self-management, the discipline that enables us to order our affairs to productive ends and to achieve our goals. They may not seem so, yet they are related in many ways and each is an extremely good habit in its own right. Indeed, given each on its own much can yet be achieved and there are plenty of examples in this book to support this. That being said, it must be emphasized that the greater fundamental argument of this enterprise, is not one of time management versus self-management, but of the addressing, harnessing and harmonizing of the interplay between the two such that extra-ordinary results ensue with application. Here, we have an interface between time management and self-management. The real issue of greater personal productivity under consideration here therefore, is not one of time management against self-management. It is instead an argument for managing the "self-management" in relation to time. It is from the proper management of this interface that extra-ordinary personal productivity is possible. This is an option that is available if we choose the path of a relationship with time. So, what is your relationship with time? What would you want it to be? What other options could there be? Let us consider mastery.

Of Mastery

Now what is Mastery? How can we attain it? Phillippa Lally, in her role as a health psychology researcher at the University College of London was a pioneer in the study of habit formation. In a study that was published in the European Journal of Social Psychology, she and her team found that it took on average between 21 and 66 days or more for a dedicated person to form a new habit to the point where this habit becomes second nature, of course depending on what habit is at stake. The harder the task, the longer the duration required. What is clear here is that habit formation takes practice, consistency and intention to succeed. In other words, automaticity is a function of repeated reinforcement of action and habit. There have been other studies that back up these claims, so the verdict is clear. The cliché "Practice makes perfect" is sound indeed.

One of my favourite authors, and a speaker of wisdom, Robin Sharma is a believer of the power of habit. He urges us to practise habit formation rituals religiously if we want to master the skills we desire for them to become second nature. Practise for 66 days, you mean?

Yes, it takes this long for us to gain mastery of a new behaviour or way of acting such that it becomes a default automatic recourse. Mr. Sharma also talks about what he calls, "Personal mastery". In a world of constant distractions, mastery of the self is such an important key to peak performance and optimal productivity that it is amazing how many of us don't pay enough attention to it. With 24-hour news flow, instant notifications and buzzing social media feeds, it can seem like every second we miss something important that we have not checked on our devices. First, we made the devices, we called it "development". Then we brought the devises into our inner space of life, and into our core existence only for the devises to own us. When it is time to work, we cannot seem to let go of the pull of trivia. Then we wonder why trivia shows up on our bank balance at the end of the pay cycle. Got it? Ya! We do not grow; our work does not grow and of course our results do not grow because trivia has taken over. We dropped the ball.

We need to take charge. In short, we need to discipline the self that is "us", regarding how, as well as how much we use and allow our modern–day "friends" to intrude into our lives. Devices are good for their purposes. The problem is that most of us don't seem able to establish and maintain the necessary boundaries that are required to keep our relationships with our gadgets healthy. We can blame the addictive nature of some of the programmes and applications embedded in these gadgets. However, it is not necessarily the fault of the gadgets, nor their creators. The blame comes back to us, for allowing ourselves to cross our own very boundaries because, yes, we do know the score with these gadgets and the fact that they tend to sap our attention and inflict damage on our productive endeavours. The question is, what are we willing to give up in order to gain back the necessary control for our greater good?

How we choose to spend our ordinary moments, determines how we choose to spend the rest of our lives; for life is nothing but an aggregation of moments well-spent, productively or otherwise. There is no magic to success in life. It all boils down to moments taken and progress made, inch by ever-adding-up inch on the path we call progress. Let's think about it. Let's ask the self: How have I in the past chosen to spend my moments? The answer lies in how your life is at this very moment.

To borrow a phrase from the theatre, when we wake up, it's "show time". What does this mean? It means time to hunt elephants. In one of his master classes on a *Mind Valley* programme, Mr Sharma spoke of the need to develop and protect our mental focus, physical energy and will power if we are to perform at our best, and optimally. He called these the "Trinity of peak performance assets". But what are these?

"Show Time", and the management of your personal energy.

Mental focus simply means concentration; the ability for you and I to direct our attention fully to whatever task we wish to accomplish. It is about intentional focus with clarity of purpose and vision and of never giving up. It is not easy. It takes real effort and commitment, and developing it may require particular changes in habits. However, it can be developed and most elite sport folks have learnt to do so. It is said that the ability to mentally focus is like training the muscles of the mind. The more practice we get, the better we become at it. Mental focus may be as simple as having the self-discipline to say "NO" to things that don't fit in your vision so you can say "Yes" to those that matter. That is to say an ability to shut off all non-essential elements to the task at hand.

One of the most effective ways of developing mental focus is what game specialists call, *Process Focus*. The claim is that by focusing on the individual steps and processes of goal attainment, one is able to narrow down and zero in on the moment and therefore to avoid being unnecessarily distracted by other enticements.

Physical energy basically refers to how healthy we are. Physical wellbeing is the basis of human health. Of course, arguably, there can be no health without mental health, but our concern here is the physical. The good news however, is that there is a strong correlation between our physical and mental health. For example, physical bodily exercise has been proven to be not only good for the body, including boosting stamina and over all energy levels, but that it also promotes mental health, helping with stress relief and promoting a general wellbeing.

Talking about energy, another author Tony Schwartz urges us to "manage your energy, not your time" and for good reason. Schwartz states that most people, including you and I that is, spend our energies chasing the wrong resource for productivity, (referring to the hours we have in the day) and that we would do better by focusing on optimizing our energies. He discusses 4 types of energy:

Physical Energy: **how medically fit we are.**

Emotional Energy: **our happy state and how well we are faring.**

Mental Energy: **how sharp and consistent our focus is on the task at hand.**

Spiritual Energy: **Whether we find meaning and purpose in our pursuits.**

Regarding physical energy, Tony Schwarz puts it best when he says that without taking care of our physical energy, we cannot build ourselves. It is therefore curious why we so often fail to take care of this resource. Most people probably take better care of their automobiles than they do their physical self in terms of the sheer care and attention allocated. For instance, we would never dream of putting sub-standard fuel in our vehicles but will gladly cut corners when it comes to feeding, all in the name of expense reduction. Faced with it, we would gladly forgo feeding in favour of fuelling our beloved wheelie. We do everything to ensure our vehicles remain in peak performance condition and not break down but usually hardly employ similar rigour and care in matters relating to our bodies.

In other words, as we have been discussing, working more, working harder and with more hours is not the answer to your productivity quest. It is good advice indeed. However, perhaps an equally important, but often over-looked factor of productivity is that which we shall call WILL POWER. Yep! It may be more important than all the collective of factors in our preparations when it comes to balancing the equation in favour of our daily productive enterprises. Call it the catalyst in our daily productivity alchemy. This is the subject of our next session. So, what is will power?

The Power of the Will

Will-power, is that which wields the balance as it were, when it is time for the proverbial rubber to hit the road and get results. Will-power is, generally, explained in terms of the capacity or ability to exercise control over an urge, usually one that competes with other desires one may have at the same time. It involves self-discipline in the face of temptation. It can save a person from trouble and propel a fellow to great heights. Unmanaged however, it can fail, for will power is not unlimited. It can be eroded over time in the face of an appropriately strong temptation. How do you deal with this? The answer is in knowing yourself.

Know your strengths, know your talents, know your desires and secret aspirations, but more importantly, know what makes you buckle at the knees. What is most likely to weaken your strongest resolve? Name it, acknowledge it, pay attention to it and work to shield yourself from it, for it is your weakest point, your exposed underbelly that is the weakest link in your personal arsenal. All your strengths must ultimately resolve to it. Wisdom demands that you remove yourself from any known temptation or whatever could likely be a sure temptation or circumstance of the kind.

Will power at its best can cause a fellow to do and achieve the unbelievable of feats. Yet, it is fragile indeed, I dare say, and unless fiercely protected, it does not last long when temptation is around. The temptation to quit, to take the easy road and the short-cut to short-circuit the very path to success is real. Every winner, every achiever, every successful person has felt this urge to quit. But it is possible to win. The difference lies in being prepared, knowing the nature of the "enemy" and not yielding. So, do yourself a favour, protect your productivity tools: Mental focus, physical energy, will power, and do not forget to save your emotions.

To better focus, remove the temptation of social media and associated distractions from your working environment. Create a work-space that supports your productivity goals. Once again, it sounds easy. It is not. But it is doable. For example, a colleague of mine informs me she uses, a soft-ware that enables her to switch off any and all distractions when she needs to focus and get work done. Try it. It may be a real saviour for you. But then again, you can just do what a low-tech fellow like me does. I tend to simply switch off my message notifications or put my phone in airplane mode, or simply turn the phone off to concentrate. Initially, I was worried that I may miss an important call or two. But I have come to realise, that callers who really want to reach me will always call back. In fact, most people I deal with have come to know and accept that they may not always reach me when THEY want to; that I am available when I AM, and not necessarily when THEY want me to be. I usually get a text notification telling me a person tried to reach me, and I schedule time to phone back. I ALWAYS phone back. This is what works for me, and my associates have come to respect my boundaries. You can find a way to secure your productive time too. Find one that works for you and those you must deal with.

But I kid you not. It does require will power and that may not be as easily accessible as you may think. Now, why is it important to protect your will power and other productive resources such as your time, your attention, focus and mental and physical energies? The simple answer is because they are assets. Yes. Just like your real estate investments, or the money in your wallet. But they are more than these. They are the potential creators of all your other assets. They are fundamental to your life, wellbeing, productivity and all else you can possibly achieve in your endeavours.

You need to protect them because not one of them is of unlimited supply. If it were so, they would be worth less. Your peak mental focus is of limited duration. For example, I can only work for about 90 minutes before I start getting distracted and wanting to do something else which I know is not in my best productive interest. Hahaha! Checking the news feed? Yep! There is evidence to show that after getting distracted in the middle of a productive flow, it may take about 20 minutes to get back on track. So, imagine all the time loss that we suffer on account of the brief glance at the news feed, the social media status, the peek at the latest notification and so on.

That is where the time goes at the end of our long day of labour. We may, feel tired at the end of the day, but not on account of productivity. What then happens? The days turn into weeks, and the weeks into months, and so on and we wonder where the time went with nothing to show for it.

To elaborate further, just like mental focus, neither physical energy nor will-power is unlimited. We can only do so much before we begin to tire physically.

Believe it or not, one of the weakest links in human achievements is will power. When people fail, it is usually not because they are incapable of meeting the demands of the task at hand. It is because they give up the will to succeed. They get tempted to "throw in" the proverbial towel. Yet that temptation is set for each and everyone, including those who would succeed. What is the difference, you may ask? It is will power. For those who ultimately succeed, will-power is the magical extra that makes it all possible over and above talent or skill and certainly luck. They get lucky because they persevere harder for longer till the end. They preserve the will to persevere in spite of daring challenges that would activate, the short-circuit of giving up, a throwing-in of the towel. But that said, how about if you were able to create more time to meet your needs?

The Time Audit:

Yes! This one is magic. You can create time if you dare. How? Read on. This right here is one magic trick for creating more time for getting things done. For a start, eliminate waste and focus, focus, and focus. There is no other way of getting around it.

Indeed, according to Psychologist William Friedman, most people tend to feel a lack of time when in fact the problem is the inefficient use of time. He says that for such people, it is a constant running about trying to get things done and time runs rather quickly. So, once again, we can see that the problem is not with "managing time" per se, but a failure to manage the self in relation to the time we have to take action on our goals.

He urges us to "create" more time for our work by making a time audit of our diaries, noting the things we seem to be spending unnecessary time on and to be ruthless in cutting back and reclaiming our asset, our time. Good advice won't you say! There is always time hidden in the pursuit of trifles, he suggests, and rightly so. However, there may also be time hidden is the manner we live our lives and the choices we make

For example, depending on your circumstances, and subject to any public health alerts, (think Covid-19 et cetera) you may be able to skip taking the wheel of your beloved automobile and catch any of the many ride-offering services available or even public transport, the train, the bus or even a car-sharing arrangement. That immediately frees up your mental focus to enable you do some work as appropriate. Depending on the length of the commute, this could be significant indeed. So, change the way you approach getting to work and presto! You have created more time for yourself to engage in "elephant hunting". You have won the day before your day at the office has begun. You are instantly ahead of the game and your productivity is heading off the charts. Fantastic, huh! How does that feel? Try it. Are you beginning to see how your task is to manage yourself and not time per se, if you want to be productive? Yes, remove the barriers you have created against the proper use of your time and you will have abundance, indeed. So, here we are, we can manage to get things done, when we choose to better manage the self in relation to our time. Try it. Another magic trick to create more time for your needs follows.

Making Magic normal.

In their book, "Make Time", Jake Knapp and John Zeratsky contend that busyness is not an excuse for lack of clarity and productivity. They remind us of the need to prioritize, to savour the "less is more" approach to productivity, and to focus on the things that matter. In short, to hunt elephants, not ants.

Warren Buffet, one of the most successful investors of all time, the Sage of Omaha, as he is affectionately referred to, tells us to learn to say "NO". A quote attributed to him has it that he says the difference between successful and very successful people is that very successful people have learnt to say "NO" to ALMOST everything. In other words, FOCUS is key to extraordinary success.

This is a man who knows a thing or two about being successful and what habits do engender success. He did not inherit his wealth, he created it and along with it created wealth for scores of hundreds of other people. Once again, saying "NO" may sound easy. It is not. It takes personal discipline, focus and will power no less. So, there you have it. If you desire more time, you can make time, create time, and you can indeed find time that lies hidden in your clutter and travia.

To begin, protect your productivity assets: your mental focus, physical energy, and your will power (stay away from the temptations of the seductive media of our time), learn to say "NO". It sounds daunting, but it is possible and you can do it. Let's try an exercise to see how you fare regarding this idea of saying "NO".

Maybe you could start by keeping a journal to note what kinds of requests, favours or demands on your time and other resources you receive for the next couple of weeks. Note how many times you say "NO" and why? How do you feel any time you say, "NO"? Guilty? Justified and elated? What do you think is your real gain? Make a note. You do not have to accept a request just because it is made of you. Surely, some people may feel let down, but hey! You are not responsible for how they feel about your truth. We each are responsible for our choices, so when we choose to ask for favours or make requests, there is the inherent risk that we may be disappointed. Our disappointment is ours alone to deal with. It is a matter of choice and responsibility, so go on, test yourself. Let's see how you get on. Good luck!

I trust you are beginning to see how to avoid a waste of your time; that you can see what additional steps and options are available to you for achieving greater productive ends than just craving for more time. Now, let's ask: who do you think you are? You are not who you think you are. You are not the master of time, and you cannot master it. You can only control yourself, and with that harness time for your greater benefit.

The fore-going are some of your options. We have so far attempted to address the premise and focus of this book, that time management per se, is a waste of your time. We have noted that our task is not to manage time, but to remove all the barriers we have set up against our proper utilization of time for our productive ends. We have discussed some of the common ways in which we fail to harness time to our advantage. We have also discussed the importance of the self and the role of self–management in personal productivity.

We have argued that time is us, and that when we think we are wasting time it is in fact ourselves, our life we waste. We have discussed the need for prioritization and the concept of 'hunting elephants, and not ants"; we have considered the need to secure, preserve and protect our productive factors such as physical energy, mental focus, and will power. We have also discussed the importance of avoiding the distractions of travia and of learning to say "NO" so we can say "YES" when it matters.

We further considered time management and health, and discussed the need for self-care. We noted that without proper self-care and our physical ability to work, no amount of time will enable us to be productive. A case in point was having time on our hands while on a sick bed. We learnt that it was possible to "create" more time for our purposes by carefully eliminating the "thieves" of time that are found in some of our daily habits, such as allowing social media to intrude into our work routine.

We also considered the notion of time across cultures and noted that our own concepts and notions of time may be more controlled and determined by the larger community we inhabit than we know and perhaps care to admit. We found that in many other cultures, time is a tool and a guide not a master.

We further considered the need to reclaim mastery of time and the requirement that we need to be in optimum health to begin to be able to deploy whatever time we have at our disposal to achieve our ends. We concluded, that time management is not about time, but about learning to manage our individual self, for it is not that time is scarce, it is that we have not the self-discipline to harness its productive potential. Let us consider in some detail, the thorny issue of social media and the impact there-of on our lives.

Stolen Time: The scourge of the social media apparatus.

Social media have come to make us feel we have thousands of fellows out there in the world who care about our every move and dance. We like the "likes" and we are disappointed when no "likes" are forth-coming regarding our very funny or well-reasoned intervention, whatever it may be. Make-belief has taken over from reality. Unfortunately, that modern-day apps and social media platforms have become major sources of distraction for many people is incontrovertible. Being "busy" is seen almost as a badge of honour, a sign of the productive self. Nothing can be further from the truth.

As we have been discussing, overcoming busyNESS and distractions require a necessary change in personal behaviour. We have to be intentional about this. There is no other way around it. The fact is, if you desire to be productive, you would have to stop being reactive to external attractions and social media: Facebook;

WhatsApp; LinkedIn; Instagram, and what have you. Of course, there is the mighty old "foe", the phone with the notifications and whatever else comes up by the minute.

In other words, we need to re-adjust and reset Time back under our firm control. We need to re-tool our default settings of behaviour that dictate mindless attraction and attention to the stimuli of social media and their apps. There are mindful and pro-active strategies for dealing with these time-suckers with their endless trappings of vacuous entertainment and offerings of gossip and excitement.

To be productive, we are urged to stay present and enjoy what is. There is a whole field of study commonly referred to as *Mindfulness* dedicated to "staying present and enjoying what is". You may want to find out more about it to see if it resonates with you. Many people attest to its usefulness.

For one thing, we cheat ourselves when we lose the present, for the constant search for stimulation can only lead to a draining of creative and personal energy. It may offer a temporary "high", yes, you read right, "a high", for the need to be constantly stimulated by social media and other distractions, is no different from that for a drug or alcohol "fix". They both work by giving us a "high" by altering our dopamine-serotonin balance in the brain. Therefore, we need to recognise and label these as such if we are to begin to remedy the situation. It is not funny. Social media is addictive, and this addiction is a clinically recognised mental health condition. It interferes with our better functioning and is therefore, a "dis-EASE" for it keeps us constantly ill at ease. We need to call it out by its proper "surname" so we can begin the process of redeeming ourselves from its hold. It is difficult in today's world of endless, algorithm-generated personalised distractions, but it is possible. It is a challenge, but it is one we cannot afford not to win.

Dear reader, losing the challenge against the modern nemesis of human progress is not an option. You and I know this. Our very survival in more senses than one depends on how we fight this insidious canker against our wellbeing. In short, we need to reconfigure our very relationship with time in the context of these everyday distractions.

For an optimal relationship, we need to develop a balanced time perspective in order to live a much happier life. Learning to shift between the different perspectives is therefore crucial for an optimal happy life, and we can learn from those who have mastered the magic of getting more out of their usual 24-hour day. We will shortly consider this next.

For now, however, let's go over a few points. As we have been discussing, in modern life, productivity is the name of the game. We are as such ever scrambling for ever-more ways of getting infinitely more out of our efforts. In other words, we see productivity as a mere direct function of time employed, and effort applied.

Cast your mind back, if you will. In school, we learn that work output is equal to Time multiplied by Effort. But while it is mathematically true for machines, it is not necessarily so for us humans. "Why?" you ask? It is because we are human beings, not work beings. We live and breathe and have other needs besides work. We are meant to accomplish much more on this side of eternity than mere work. It takes more than work to make life worthwhile. As we have discussed already, there are ways to attain this, including for example, using the power of leverage in its various forms.

To be more productive therefore, it is usually not necessary to expend more time or effort. What is required is a paradigm shift in our approach, an enlargement of our "context", an expansion of our mental frame of what we believe is possible, as Robert Kiyosaki explains in his book, *Rich Dad's Retire Young, Retire Rich*. In other words, we need a different Time by Effort equation. What is more, this is different for different people. Everybody's variable is different. The time and effort you require to achieve your "A" grade is different from mine. Does this ring true? Do you remember your school days? Yes? The grades were not necessarily in proportion to how much effort and time you variously put in. You may have stayed up all night revising for that test, while your friend slept the night away but still managed top marks. How do you explain that? Being productive is not all about expending more and more time and effort. It requires a new set of behaviour; a paradigm shift in mind-set and a willingness to do other than has always been done to-date. It calls for a moving away from the popular way; the *this-is-how-it-is-done* method, and to embrace change that is personal, wholesome, valid and springs out of our personal needs and wants, and the demands of the dream burning inside of each of us that only we can, and must fulfill.

The need is for a new learning; a self-introspection; an inventory of how we have related to time so far and to realise that we could be doing better. Thankfully, we do not need to reinvent the proverbial wheel. There are lessons we can and must learn from others who have been where we are now, and have made the transition to a successful relationship with time. Learning to embrace the needed shift in our self-time relationship is the subject of our next chapter.

Chapter Five

"If you go about your business like everybody else, you will end up like everyone else, so observe the crowd and take the uncharted path."

A shifting of the Paradigm: On doing things differently, and the rewards of learning from others.

In *15 Secrets Successful People Know About Time Management*, Kevin Kruse shows us what we could all achieve by following some simple but effective methods of the very top performers in various fields of endeavour. One thing is true: we can all learn to achieve more with less time and effort. However, we must first be willing to un-time ourselves, to unlearn the ingrained habits and notions of old that less than serve our best intentions and replace these with new and effective skills. We must change our unhealthy relationship with time; our view of productivity and achievement and what it means to be successful.

We need to begin to define success for ourselves based on our own *examined* needs and wants and what it is that makes us feel fulfilled, and not just buy into the rhetoric of the generic socially prescribed, one-size-for –all definition of success which only means more, and more, and more and more and more of what we may already have attained. The irony is that usually, beyond *enough*, whatever we may be clamouring for actually begins to have very little meaning for us.

But how do we begin to individually define what success, wealth and productivity are, and look like to, and for us? We all can't have the same purpose and therefore we must eschew the temptation to buy into the generic construct of the equation: (Success=Money) unless it is what we personally choose for ourselves. But even if this is our individual definition, we only need but look at the world according to Covid-19 to realise that soul-less money in and of itself counts for very little in real life and life-obliteration situations. But I digress.

The call is to embrace a new paradigm of success, wealth and productivity that has at its core, the reality that less (with a soul) can indeed be more, (let's call it compassionate wealth), a cliché, yes, but true non-the-less. Indeed, of what we do already have, we can by properly deploying the same, achieve more of that which we desire.

Kruse reminds us that time is our most precious endowment and we must therefore spend it wisely. Good advice, you would agree. But for most of us, we for the most part don't get to spend our time. Yes, you read that right. Our time is spent for us. How? As we have already noted it could for instance be through all that daily feed of social media and the demands of others, friends, family and associates, on our time.

So, let's ponder this question: How much time do you have for yourself and the things that you truly care about? How much control do you really think you have on your time, day-by-day? Here is an exercise for you. Go on; have a go at it.

Mastering your 1440

Let's do it this way. Take a blank sheet of paper. Start from the morning. You know how many hours you have in a day. Start from the day of the week you were born (just to remind yourself that your time is different from mine and the next fellow). Do you remember we spoke about personal time? Go on and chart a log of how you have tended to use your time in the last couple of weeks. Do try hard and remember your days and nights. How much of those hours were devoted to your own important pursuits, those things you really care about?

We each have 1440 minutes per day, yes, that is all, 18400 seconds per day. And yes, *all* is an awesome lot of resource. More importantly, how we progress in this life is ultimately a function of how effectively we use this daily gift. It comes down to our personal habits as they relate to Time. Whether we choose to slumber or labour, Time goes on its journey, as it should. Productivity, is also a matter of setting priorities. As you would remember, we discussed elsewhere about hunting elephants and not ants.

As we have discussed elsewhere, the trick is to prioritise the 20% of your actions that yield the 80% of your results. In other words, our ability to set the right priorities for our time use is the single most important determinant of success and productivity. But of course, we must first determine what success looks like to us.

Another "not-so-secret" that Kruse shares with us is the need to plan and schedule specific time for our priority list of items. Your usual list of lists is of no use at all if all it does is remind you of what needs to be done without the how and when it gets done. You must also know what resources are needed to accomplish the tasks. That is to say, we must schedule accountability with our tasks. Each task must be accompanied by an accountability plan and a schedule for completion. That is how you get productive and do more with less hustle. But then sometimes other factors can interfere, like stress.

Now, stress is a big ONE. It can creep up on us, and wreak havoc if we let it. We must not and cannot ignore it. We do so at our peril. Stress is important in the productivity equation because it threatens to derail our efforts. It correlates negatively with our productive energies and must therefore be checked. But how can we deal with stress in our work life? Some experts suggest relaxation exercises and practices such as Meditation and Mindfulness. I find that under extreme stress, physical exercise is a saviour. It calms my mind and fills me with renewed impetus for action. But there is more. How about some Joy?

Planning for joy

Take time to do fun things; things that make you feel alive. You deserve it. If you don't, stress will show itself in other ways in your life: Being grumpy, quarrelsome, being unhappy and unpleasant for no apparent reason and even suffering the onset of unexplained physical and psychological ailments. These will compromise your ability to execute your neatly thought-out productivity plan. Yes, the body will always win, so treat it better than you did last time, always. Now, what about the mind?

Freeing your mind

Have you ever woken up in the middle of the night with a brilliant idea that wouldn't let you sleep? (That was your brain under the stress of burning ideas). What did you do? Best remedy? Write, write, write and write. Write down your idea. Your brain will thank you for that. Your brain is designed for thinking, not for holding on to stuff. It is a thinking box, not a storage bin. What this means is that the more we clear our mind's inbox, the better space it will have to generate better ideas. That is one of the best ways to become productive in solving problems.

Sir Richard Branson, Founder and Chairman of the Virgin Group, is known for carrying a note pad with him almost everywhere he goes. Now, this is a man who has achieved a lot in his time and in different spheres of enterprise. How else do you think he manages to attain all the various achievements in the diverse fields of endeavour he and his team are engaged in, from catering to Virgin Brides to space travel on a Virgin Galactica, and even an ocean bed expedition? Harness your ideas by writing them down. How productive is that!

Note also that the very best of the most successful are also reputed to be efficient with the time they spend on meetings. So, if you want more time to do what is important, take control of your time when it comes to meetings. Say "No" to meetings unless absolutely necessary. There is a famous law concerning this. It is Parkinson's Law of Triviality. It states that work expands to fill the time available for its completion. The law would suggest that meetings tend to be a waste of time by often being inefficient with time. They would drag on over trivial matters just eating way time. The very best of productive persons know this. Therefore, do place a premium of your time and skills. You don't have to do everything, because you can't.

Who else can do your job?

Leverage your skills, delegate work to achieve more. Put another way, "clone" yourself, to do more, achieve more, attain more and get more out of your competence. It is said that a successful person is one who has a successor. So, you want to be successful? Build a successor. Teach and mentor others to do what you do to the very best of their abilities. Empower them to achieve, to soar, make yourself redundant to free yourself and your time to do other things, to achieve more, to dream bigger, to become more of what you could be beyond your wildest dreams and enjoy more, because you can. Being successful requires a more expansive approach to life and work. It is not all about working 8 hours. We shall next consider the traditional 8-hour workday, and why it sets us up to deceive ourselves and to fail.

Many of these ideas shared here are not necessarily new. A lot has been written and said about them variously from the time of ancient African civilization to Grecian and Roman times, all the way to the present. However, as wisdom would have it, after trying for so long and so hard to upend the natural course of the productive day and redefine productive success, we seem to have begun to come round to acceptance of these truths, and the ideas themselves are beginning to gain currency as we have begun to realize that productivity entails more than long hours of labour. Here are some perspectives on the subject.

Why the 8-hour workday doesn't work.

How many hours of the employer's paid-for 8-hour day do we really spend in top productivity? Have you ever considered this? As we have sought to explain elsewhere, the industrial revolution is to blame for seeking to turn us humans into machines, albeit with our very complicity. True? Yes! First, we established the regime to get more out of the labour of our fellow wo/man, not realizing that that fellow wo/man is, us. Indeed, it bears asking again: whoever works for 8 hours and believes s/he has produced 8 hours of honourable good?

That we go to work for 8 hours and produce 8 hours' worth of results must the greatest deceptive secret of all time. What I am saying here is that your employer pretends to have your best interest at heart and captures your 8 most productive hours of the day; you go in and at the end of the day, you pretend to have offered the employer 8 hours of your very best focus, concentration, attention and energy. It is just not possible that we are able to offer that degree of productivity. We are human. Other factors are more important in the productivity equation than mere time and effort. We have discussed this in part elsewhere. Let us have a look at it in more detail from another perspective.

So, now that we accept that perhaps, we may be better served by re-imagining our concepts of productivity and the role of time, the question begs to be asked: So, what options do we have? Let us recap the arguments so far. We have considered concepts such as: What is time? what does time mean to you and I individually? We have assessed time as an agent of work; time as a resource; time as a master; time as being relative; time as an absolute entity; time as a social construct and it being abstract. We mentioned time to be a healer; we considered time as an enabler and we discussed the need to break from the shackles of time in order to be truly productive. We said being productive required much more than just getting work done. We concluded that we needed to break from the shackles of time and to readjust our personal relationships with time if we desire better results from our endeavours. Here's a little exercise for you.

Consider the following piece:

What does time mean to you?

Time, a friend yet a foe we may make it.

Time, the wise counsellor, and yet, it may fool us.

Time is everything and yet an illusion;

Time: a nothing without human enterprise.

Time is what it is; whatever we choose to make it;

Make of it; with it; by it; through it; in spite of it; because of it; a celebration worthy of it.

So, what does time mean to you?

Yes, so what does time mean to you? A simple question it may be. But unless we have a clear understanding of what it is time is to us, it will be difficult to establish the necessary healthy relationship with time that is fundamental to the very productive success that we seek in our labours and personal life.

Our current attitudes and relationships with time is the result of habit. To have an alternative relationship, will take a change in habit. Success is but a culmination of the results of great helpful habits practised consistently. Therefore, if we seek to achieve success in our relationship with time, we must choose those habits that have been proven to work and practise them consistently. Yes, we must practise them not a few times, or once in a while, but CONSISTENTLY. No one ever became successful overnight. There is always the slugging that went into the eventual attainment of the object. We need to always remember that.

So how may we proceed? Like all great achievements, we must be intentional about what it is we want and it must start with self-knowledge, knowing what drives us, what our core values are and whether we indeed have the temperament to stick it out to the glorious end. It is very easy to start things; what is not so easy is sticking with the plan through all the difficulties that are bound to show up and test our resolve. If we have had that discussion already with our person, the self that is, we would be ready when the time comes, and we will say, "I am no quitter". We would have the courage to press on to victory. This is the very essence of success. It is the quality that distinguishes the successful from the failed enterpriser. Let's call it the *"Stick-with-it-ness"*, the courage to stick with the plan and slug it out, whatever "it" is. So first get to know yourself.

But what is the self? Let's do the following exercise to find out. Ready? Answer the following questions for yourself.

Exercise: *Knowing me*

- Who are you?
- What kind of life do you desire for yourself now and forever?
- How do you hope to attain this?
- Why is time important to you?
- Why does it matter?
- What is your personal relationship with time like?
- What are your personal productivity habits?
- Why is this important?
- Do you have a personal productivity ritual? What is it? Does it matter?
- What are your personal beliefs about time and time management?
- Do you have a "big idea" you desire to achieve? Describe it.
- What is your plan for achieving this?
- What is your daily routine like? Does it move you closer to your end game and final result?

Hold on to your insight. It is valid for you. If you are happy with the way things are… then great! Congratulations! If not, you know what to do.

The Virtue of Having a Personal Daily Ritual:

In his book, "On the shortness of life", Seneca the philosopher, enjoins us to "live each day as if it were a whole life" and why not? It may well be our only chance. Remember, only hope intervenes for our tomorrow.

Consider a ritual like this. It is my personal daily ritual: I call it my WREP protocol. It stands for Work, Rest, Entertainment and Personal development. I endeavour to do activities that fulfill elements of each category each day. Yours may be different. If you don't have one, I urge you to develop one for yourself. For one thing, a personal daily ritual keeps you focused. It automates your day in terms of what you need to do broadly, to meet your goals. It ensures that you have covered all necessary aspects of your life. Without a personal ritual, we are likely to overly concentrate on one or a few aspects of our life goal to the exclusion of other areas. But as we all know, success is about balance. It is a juggling enterprise. You cannot afford to drop any of the balls, so to speak. Indeed, if you are really interested in developing a better life-work balance, there's a programme called *Lifebook*, developed by Jon and Missy Butcher available on Mind Valley. You may check if it's something that resonates with you. It did with me.

Anyway, in my WREP protocol, work would be that activity that would bring in the cash to pay the bills at the end of the month; rest means I have a good nap during the day; entertainment would be anything that would make me laugh or at least take my mind off work and other pressures, and that genre is broad indeed and then comes personal development. I make sure to exercise each day and to read a good book or listen to or watch personal development materials by experts I admire, to improve both my physical and mental self, and knowledge.

This is how I balance my day. Once I have accomplished elements in these categories I feel successful. I feel that I have won the day; and guess what, such wins add up in the end, always have and always will. Find your own balance. You must do all that needs to be done without sacrificing any aspect of your life. Now let's assume you have done the above exercise and now know thyself. So, what's left? Let's see next.

Chapter Six

Convenience is not promised on the road to success.-NB-D

What's left?

So now, what's left? Congratulations, you made it this far. We are almost at the end. In this chapter, we shall take a look at some of the habits and practices that have proven beneficial in the real world for real people in their effort at getting more done in the time we all have allocated to us by nature; our 1440 minutes in the time it takes the sun to rise and set on our day. Well, come along.

Here are some general tips from some of those who live success regarding working smart. This is important because it shows there's a plan for success. It is not theory. It is practical. We all have the same 24 hours in a day. All our struggles concern trying to get more out of these hours. In other words, we struggle against time. However, as we have been discussing, with this orientation, it's a struggle we are ultimately bound to lose before the end we seek.

But success, however we define it, is not about managing time per se, but about self-organization which involves habits, routine, self-care, relationships fostered and nurtured, and how we create and use the synergy of community that is available to us. In short, there's the hard way and then the smart path involving proven strategies. Working smart will yield more success with less resources and "hustle", in a shorter span of time. In effect it's like creating more time out of your 24-hour allotment to do all the things you want and to give yourself free time out of life to enjoy the proverbial fruits of your labour.

I believe you have heard this saying: failing to plan is planning to fail. Sure! And so, plan we must. But most people think of big plans with large time scales and horizons: 2-year, 5-year and 10-year plans that have incredible schemes of success that we can visualize. That is very seductive indeed. We feel really good watching the movie of our success play in our minds. However, while the end may look easy, it is not always that easy to figure out how such monumental success is achievable. The "What" is the easy part, what is usually not so easy is the "How'. We all know what we want. Our task then is to figure out HOW to get our WHAT.

It may seem easy. The reality however, is that success, no matter how grand, is attained through the execution of simple daily actions. So, yes set that big goal to challenge you. But also get to work on the simple daily "boring", tedious pieces of stuff that are the brick and mortar of your *Success Cathedral*, your goal monument. For starters, have a routine, make a daily plan of activities you will need to execute to move you each day, inch by ever increasing inch towards your goal fulfilment.

To restate a point discussed earlier,

'If you want to be successful, live each day as if it were a whole life'.

I refer to this again because it is the core of successful living. Therefore, have a plan for each day; execute it well without excuses. What do you gain from brushing your teeth daily? Nothing? Nothing apparently. But over time, you gain healthy teeth. If you doubt, try the opposite. So, it is with your daily habits and plans in the ultimate scheme of your big 10-year dream or whatever time-scale yours is on.

If you desire your dream that badly get to work: make a daily, weekly, monthly and yearly plan. Plan and execute each day's activity and task like it is your sole bridge to your goal attainment, your success, because, guess what… IT IS.

However, to have the peace and quiet to focus and work on your plan, you have to recognize and deal with those suckers in your life. D-I-S-T-R-A-C-T-I-O-N-S. I am talking of:

-Designed

-Instruments

-Secretly

-Taking away

-Real-A-C-T-I-O-N-S

-Creativity

-Time

-Investments

-Over all and

-Never Stopping.

DISTRACTIONS steal your progress so:

Turn off your phone, if you must. Well, at least put it on silence so those notifications don't "eat up" your focus and attention. In fact, given the power of the phone and how we have managed to make it become a core of our lives, it is not always easy to be without the beloved item. But hey! You bought it. You own it. Don't allow any role switching. You are the master. Act as such. You get to decide when, for how long, and how you get to interact with that sucker of time, energy, attention and focus. More importantly, no matter how you choose to use your time, do not allow other people's agenda to consume your focus, attention, time nor energy whether through phone or physical presence.

To do this, you have to start by setting clear boundaries regarding how you treat your day. Communicate this plan firmly and clearly to all your associates and family, and importantly, stick to it. Learn to deal with the initial discomfort your new found assertive self may cause with those who have everything to gain from the old state of affairs, at your expense; at the expense of your dreams, aspirations and a better life for yourself. Go on, set a new scheme, unleash new rules and create firm boundaries to guide you for the road ahead.

Remember, you can never win your day by giving up your valuable time and energy for the sake of all else but your goals. Think about it. Do yourself a favour, go ahead and set some firm boundaries and don't worry about who gets upset. You are claiming your life back and respecting your needs. You owe it to yourself. If you don't value and respect your time, how do you expect others to? Respect yourself and your time, and don't allow yourself to cross your own boundaries. It matters a lot. Yes, it does, more than you may think.

We spoke about dealing with the phone. Now if your business relies on the phone, that may be an exception but even that, you will be more effective if you plan your out-going calls and screen in-coming ones to ensure you are only prioritizing the most important tasks. All others can wait. Do you really have to answer the phone because someone is at the other end? Not necessarily. These days we are able to tell whoever that fellow at the other end is, and so can decide whether the interruption may be warranted. Think of the damage a loss in focus, concentration and flow that a single answering of the phone can do to your productivity. How do you feel about that? Let your answer be your guide.

In short, we are saying here, that we need to take back control of our interactions with this tool. Yes, you read right. Your beloved phone is only a tool. See and use it as such. Answering the phone in the middle of getting other things done is the classic multi-tasking behaviour. Once upon a time, such behaviour was hailed and even actively encouraged. Hiring managers would actually specify multi-tasking as if it were a super skill set, and indeed, many people bought into it. It was, hey! Look at me. I can do this and this and that and those too, while performing these and those and that in addition. Now, we know better. You cannot be effective without focus.

There's good sense in the wisdom of the old saying, "Jack of all trades master of none". I quite like the Chinese version, "If you chase two rabbits, you will lose both". That is much clearer, I think. You could actually go out and literally try it out for yourself. Focus is the foundation of mastery, so keep your focus on the task at hand. Everything else can and must wait (unless of course a life is at stake. In that case, you will know to dial 999). You will be a hero for that. Life comes first, now, forever has been, and always will.

Just remember:

Your focus and attention determine your output, not how much time you spend apparently doing a task. So, when you sit down to work, get working. Focus all your energies and attention on the task at hand. You will amaze yourself.

The truth is managing your attention is more important to your success and productivity than managing your time. It's quite a surprise why many of us do otherwise. Results are everything so judge your efforts by the results not your time. Great results take effort and sustained focus.

Consider the Chinese bamboo. It is said to take five years to sprout out of the ground. Imagine watering this bamboo for 5 long years with no apparent result, especially if you can't even be sure whether it is dead or still alive. But like the dedicated trusting gardener, you continue to believe in the process. You continue to water and have faith in the process of its life form to grow. Then after 5 years, hurray! It shows its "face": a tiny peek through the earth. Hallowed ground has broken, and like the cliché goes, the rest is history. To the, world you may have just struck it "lucky". Good on you! But every man or woman makes his or her own luck through grit, dedication, focus and the cultivation of the unyielding entrepreneurial spirit that says, "I am no quitter" and by staying true to the dream, never yielding to the pangs of defeat; whether by way of failing energy, sweat, self-doubt or mockery by others regarding lack of what it takes in the moment. You won because you still kept on pushing and watering the cause; you won because you did believe. You win again and again because you follow the formula; you trust the process.

So, you have your bamboo out of the ground. It is a little weakling of greenery. But magic happens, and after another 5 to 6 weeks that little sprout of a twig, is about 80 or 90 feet tall. Now that is some magic, won't you say? Except you know better. Magic is the result of consistency of effort, belief, dedication, patience and trust in the process. So, if you desire success, set your compass; pick your goal; get to work; be patient; have some faith; invest in your mission, including in your good self. The potential is within; it shall not be long. Get ready for your magic!

Indeed, we can take heart that our small, tiny, daily efforts never go to waste. Nothing we do in enterprise is in vain, if we have a plan to it. So, measure your success by your results; apply that effort and keep it consistent. Consistency is key; time is nothing by and of itself.

But developing consistency does not always come easily. So, as discussed elsewhere, have a routine. A routine takes out the argument you would otherwise sometimes have to have, with your best intentions regarding, "should I?" and "should I not?" With a routine, when it is time to act, you just do it. You don't make excuses because you have had the conversation with yourself already and made the decision. So, as we are beginning to see, routines keep us consistent with our plans. They anchor us to our path towards the fulfilment of our goals. Therefore, by all means, have your 10-year plan. Set goals and break them into yearly, monthly, weekly and daily activities and then create that routine to keep you on track. Review your progress at the end of the day, week, month and year and see what magic looks like. But you must be INTENTIONALLY consistent. If your bamboo needs watering at dawn, noon and evening, you cannot choose to skip say a morning routine because you slept late the night before and woke up late. Big success invariably requires great management capacities to steward it.

Being consistent may not always be convenient. But then *convenience is not promised on the road to success.* So, stick to the routine. Trust the process. You cannot go wrong. You may just surprise yourself. But sometimes one needs more than mere consistency to succeed. People matter. We are the result of our social connections and interactions. It is therefore wise to cultivate good community. It may just be the leverage that enables your dreams to take off. This is the focus of our next section.

The Virtue of Building Strategic Relationships

Perhaps one of the most under-rated determinants of success is "relationships". I am not talking about having a thousand friends on social media. I refer to relationships that confer leverage to your goals and put fuel in your tank for the journey. These are collaborative, strategic relationships. Get to know and be with people who have dreams and are taking action. Offer your help, know-how and services. Be useful to them and in time you will be able to leverage these relationships to win your cause. It is a win-win-win. So, seek to be useful to people on a mission. They in turn will be useful to you. You will achieve more in less time than you can through solo effort. Nobody succeeds alone; always remember that. Finally:

ALWAYS finish what you start; it is the only way to achieve anything.

Of Self-investment and Success

We have so far been discussing how time management is a waste of your time and all the other things that matter more than that. In the end it is how far you have come that matters. It is how much you have grown since you last checked in with yourself. It is what you do, have done, and continue to do with your 24-hour ration in terms of your own growth that counts. So, no matter what you think about the subject, invest in yourself. Personal development is at the core of any achievement. The important thing is to never stop learning. Read, take relevant courses, and never stop being curious. Personal growth is LIFE itself. That is success, ultimately. Think about it.

On showing up with your whole self

Have you ever taken the time to consider this? How would spending time at work, furiously trying to "manage" the 70% of your waking hours that you spend at work make you any productive if you are disengaged from the task at hand? You tell me. Yes, we spend 70% of our waking hours, not with family, friends, on self-improvement, sleeping or doing preferred fun things, but at work, (if we are fortunate enough to have one, given these trying economic times). It is because being in possession of employment is such good fortune that we must, and need to bring our whole selves to the work we have, because it is a real possession in these times, and we cheat ourselves for being only fractionally present in our tasks.

Showing up with our whole self to the task means committing our full presence of mind, attention and focus because success demands nothing short of full commitment and focus. We short-change ourselves otherwise. When we show up with our whole self, we can potentially achieve great productive ends, and we do so efficiently, with less stress and strain on body and soul. More importantly, when we do not attend with our whole self, we waste time, the time we are eager to manage; the employment time, those precious 8 hours in the day but also ultimately, we waste ourselves. We do because:

Time is US, individually, personally, collectively…and what a waste of LIFE itself! Think about it. If we are to be productive, how we show up to our work matters. However, it is also true that sometimes how we show up at the work place is not only determined by our personal life issues such as, what stresses we have at home or in the community. It is sometimes a factor of the very organizational culture of the place we inhabit as our work environment.

Studies consistently show that many people hate the work they do that feeds them, puts a roof over their head and gives them a sense of purpose to face the day. Some even dread going in to work on occasion. There is a reason for the so-called Monday Blues syndrome, I guess. If you don't like the culture of the organization you work for, move. Don't be afraid to change the situation. It can only get better because you took action. Not acting and remaining in the situation is no way to honour your talents and yourself.

Life is too precious to allow it to go waste. Don't be complicit. You deserve better. You know it. Do what it takes. Go on. There's gold at the end of the hole. Step sideways, pull out, do whatever you must to better your lot and honour yourself. Just don't stop prospecting for your golden opportunity. It's yours to take. All it takes is to leave your comfort zone; brave the odds and seek a better outcome for yourself.

Surely your dream awaits but first, you must wake up to your current reality. But how can you dream if you are afraid to fall asleep? If you desire better, slumber out of your current reality and awaken with a new vision.

Chapter Seven

Harness your moments; know that time is you, and it is not time you waste, but yourself. -NB-D

And Finally:

There has been a lot to consider and ponder. But it all boils down to you, your good self and how much investment you are ready to make towards the realisation of your dreams. Time is only a tool to use. But it is not time that shapes our mortal and material fortunes. It is "us". It is what qualities, mind sets, and skills we bring to the application of the time we have that creates our reality; the result; the success or otherwise. So, here is what I know. Stop fretting about time and time management. Make yourself valuable to the market place. You will command more per unit of your "Time", so to speak. Start investing in yourself and the skills and qualities that will enable you to strip away all the obstacles and challenges that stand in the way of your proper utilisation of the instrument you call "Time". That is your sole task. But, whilst at it…

Enjoy The Ride

Have you seen the film, *"The Titanic"?* Here is a short summary. The now famous ship was a luxury British-made steam cruiser that sank on its maiden voyage in the early hours of April 15, 1912 after it struck an iceberg. History has it that more than 1500 people died in the accident. But what interests me here is what I consider as a metaphor for living: What that whole Titanic cruise and the eventual disaster can and does teach us about life and why it matters that we live it and do it well and with deliberate gusto, plan and effort and to be sure to be happy and joyful and grateful for each day, and to especially enjoy the ride through life. Gratitude brings joy. One cannot at once be grateful and lack joy. Being joyful is not about having achieved all your goals; it is about acknowledging your progress; how far you have come and enjoying what is. There is research to the effect that feeling joyful can get one through difficult times. To quote Mrs. Obama in one interview, "Because you planned for joy, it means joy is coming". You know this. This knowledge, the expectation, is such a potent force of energy bringing hope and courage to your days leading to the planned JOY event or act. JOY is good for your health. Embrace it.

In praise of self-care: Time Management and your health.

I bet you are asking what time management has to do with your health and healthcare for that matter? Well, for starters, if you are in ill-health you can kiss good-bye to all the time management techniques or hacks and whatever latest fad may be in the field. Being ill means essentially that you are, "toast". You need to be in optimum health to even begin to deploy the essential productivity skills that we have been discussing so far. Therefore, no matter what you do, do not neglect yourself. It is the only intervention you can make on behalf of body and soul in pursuit of the good life.

It is YOU the self serves, but are you serving the self? I sincerely hope that when you choose, your choices serve your highest self and wellbeing, for the body will always win; so too will the soul.

You had better get on their side. Who doesn't like the company of a winner! I do. Surely you do too. Your task is cut out for you then.

The following are a few approaches to self-care:

- **The Leverage of being yourself. Be unapologetically and authentically you:**

For starters, pretence is the ultimate insult to the self. "Why?" you ask? It is because it is a lie to the self in any other way and you know it. To be lied to is to be told in other ways that you are not intelligent; that you do not and would not know the difference from the truth. You know the truth when you pretend to be what you are not. You get the point? Respect the self. Be you. Be authentically you; be you in all your weirdness and imperfections and tears and feelings of uncertainty and so on, because that is the only way to find fulfilment.

- **The Leverage of loving yourself enough to not disrespect your wishes and feelings and longings:** Self-respect is non-negotiable. It is off the table, no matter the odds. In other words, I am saying, no matter what you choose to do in this life, in all your labours and aspirations, never lose your dignity. It's all a man or woman has got. Without dignity, nothing matters. Why would you strip yourself of your dignity? So, be unapologetically you. In the words of the famous Irish writer, Oscar Wilde, "Be yourself everyone else is taken". Remember that.

- **The Leverage of saying what you mean and meaning what you say:**

In our communications with others, we tend to buy into the social drug of "politeness" or as the term goes, "political correctness". A rose by any other name is still a rose with its thorns and smell and aesthetic delights; so is a spade by any other name. I am not advocating rudeness. Successful communication is about saying what is on your mind by minding how you say it. That is to say, it is not WHAT is said so much as HOW it is said. Lying by failing to say what needs to be said; what you mean to say; saying YES when you really mean to say NO, is such a low sad lie firstly to the self and then the other. It does grave disservice to both you and your listener. What a waste of opportunity; an opportunity to assert your dignity. Indeed, it undermines the dignity of the verbal intercourse itself. Who wants to be lied to? So go on, say what you mean. People will ultimately respect you for that.

When we are little children, we may indeed have little choice. The dictates of our socio-cultural environment may upstage our better self and we may not have the resources to act in the direction of our wants and needs and desires. That can be forgiven. What is worrying is that most of us fail to break out of this conditioning even as fully functioning, independent adults, and keep on acting in ways that undermine our greater good and even dignity.

Well, here is Lisa Nichols a communications expert at a Mind Valley event (and I love this):

> **"... some of you are still asking for permission... and sometimes you have to stop asking for permission. And it's time to give the world notice... now it's time to play full out."**

Yep! You are enough. You do not need permission to be yourself. So, go on and just BE and see magic happen: Abundance in health, love, relationships, confidence and self-worth. What more can anyone ask for? Lying takes too much effort. Eschew it. I say live your truth.

Oh! by the way, this is all in the context of our time management too. What a waste of your precious time saying things you do not mean, to satisfy folks you have no respect for! (If you did respect them, you would not tell them lies, we have established that). If you are concerned about productivity, pay attention; be effective in your daily communication and engagements. Do not waste your life (time) lying to yourself, and to others. Lies achieve little ultimately. Everyone comes off the worse for it-deceived, resentful, and vengeful.

- **The Leverage of Learning to ask for help:** If you need help, ask. In spite of what it may seem nowadays, the world is still filled with goodness and good people; many people are happy to oblige, if only you have the courage to ask.

- **The Leverage of saying sorry and meaning it:** It takes courage to admit one is wrong. But it also shows strength of self, integrity and character. It shows you care about the relationship and are secure enough in your own sense of self to admit that you indeed

fell short of your own high standards. People will respect you for that. It's a bonus, because by admitting you are wrong, you have shown self-respect. That's enough. It's all that really matters.
More importantly, it will free your very soul of the otherwise negative emotions and energies that tend to swell up with guilt on the conscience, and …who needs that?

- **The Leverage of disagreeing, and saying so:** If you don't agree, say so. Say, "I don't agree. You would have made your point. You may be right or wrong, but that is your point made. It is enough. You will only resent yourself otherwise, if you harbour your disagreement. It will fester and run and make you sour and ugly and even more disagreeable. If you pretend to agree when you don't, people will notice that too. Ultimately, they will mark you down in their books on the respect scale.

- **The Leverage of not understanding something, and saying so:** If you don't understand something, say so. Just say, simply, "I don't understand". It is not only a powerful sign of confidence, but of intelligence too. By asking for clarification and further explanation, you are actually showing the other, that you are interested in whatever the subject or topic under discussion is, and what the other has to say. People feel validated when we show interest in them and their ideas. They will be happy to repeat or reframe their pitch for your benefit, and guess what, theirs too. You will get a better, clearer understanding of what is at stake; what it is they have to say, and what their real intended meaning is. Don't be surprised to learn after explanation that what you might have thought was the message, was not it at all. The lesson here is not to ever make assumptions. Do not impose "understanding". Seek clarification. Clarity saves TIME. At the very least, it will save confusion. Confusion can be costly in more ways than one. You certainly do not have TIME for that and your time is precious, use it well. This is just one other way of managing your time by managing yourself, your habits, and your attitudes, your tendencies and your ways. In other words, what I am saying to you, and sincerely trust you appreciate, is that your **"TIME management" is all about your SELF-management.** Nothing can replace that.

- **The Leverage of Reserving Judgement:** Be careful what you make of what others say or do. In whatever situation, if you think you agree, hold on to the nod of the head; if you think you disagree, hold on to that side-ways shake of the head. Give yourself a chance to hear a fellow out and leave time to process the feed from your senses. As the saying goes, the eyes look, but it is the brain that sees. Listen more, speak less is a virtue of a saying. In all things, seek to understand the perspective of the other as a fundamental first. This is neither new nor original.

Ancient cultures have preached it over the centuries, from African Kingdoms, to Greek, Roman and Eurasian states. Reserving judgement is golden. As Epictetus, the Greek philosopher has said, "We have two ears and one mouth so that we may listen twice as much as we speak." There is also a general saying that it is not what enters us (what others say or do to us; or what we witness) that defiles us (causes us trouble or pain), but what comes out of us (what we say, or do in relation or reaction to what is done or said to us). So, do take care of yourself, your words and actions. Never you allow another's actions and words to affect or dictate your behaviour. Silence is golden; speech is silver, is a cliché but it is well worth repeating. You know that too. Heed it. It's good advice. Your time is precious. Do not spend it creating pain in your life. You deserve better, so do better, because you can. Yes, even if it is just because you CAN. You owe it to your better self.

- **The Leverage of Being grateful for the Time you have:** So, you think time is scarce; you don't have enough time; 24 hours barely honour your needs? Not so. Time has always been enough. There's always enough to do what needs to be done, when it needs to be done, provided desire and intention drive our actions. We must be intentional in our use of time, if we truly mean to honour and show gratitude to the time we do have. Being intentional means, knowing what is an effective, and warranted use of our time resource in any given situation. Take care of all the little ways you dishonour time, and time will reward you with abundance for your efforts at having a good go at your goals.

Respecting and honouring the time you have, is how you show up in gratitude for life, yes, your life, for time is life and the time you have is the life you have got. Think about it. We are not wasting time when we fail to honour it as the single most important, and sacred resource available to us; we waste our life. We are all on timers. It sounds cheesy, doesn't it? But it's true. No one knows when the energy in our individual little timers will run out, so we had better make good use of our now.

Why complain about the apparent dearth of minutes when you can use these to accomplish some useful thing for your cause? Be grateful for the moments you do have to do whatever your focus is on. Let the moments count; create memories. Ultimately, our lives are but memories for in the end, memories will be all that will be left. Make yours count.

- ***The Leverage of Knowing the difference between Integrity and Honesty and acting accordingly:***

Sometimes we make wrong choices and we regret. While nobody may know if we didn't own up, Honesty makes us own up to our fault perhaps due to regret and the prick of the conscience.

Integrity however, secures us from choosing the wrong path in the first place because we have had that conversation with our inner self, based on our values as to who we are, who we want to be and our respect for the self and our dignity. Our integrity is a measure of, and an encapsulation of our undivided self. We are the first to know if we have done right or wrong. Nobody else does. It is enough that we know what we have or have not done. In this conversation, we have concluded, that there are things and behaviours that are beneath our personal dignity and so we will neither yield to their temptation, nor lend our energies to them. Ultimately, because we have already determined what the bottom line is regarding these issues and circumstances our moral compass steers us clear of engaging in things that will impinge upon our dignity and the wholeness of the self. When we pursue and honour integrity, we are choosing to preserve our wholeness, our undivided, not-to-be divided self.

So, choose honesty, but beyond that, strive for integrity. It's a wholesome self; and it is yours to claim. Therefore, choose integrity; keep your word. A wo/man's word is all s/he has got sometimes. Keeping your word is respecting yourself; keeping your word, will buy you trust; trust will afford you credit in people's bank of goodwill, and this will enable you to do, attain, and achieve things that you could never otherwise on your own, with your own resources, with all the time in the world do.

But just in case you still think time management is your ticket to productivity? Think again. Being worthy of trust can have a more profound impact on your abundance than you can ever dream of, and so, dear reader, no matter the odds, remember to keep your word. Trust is a rare but golden currency in these times of lying and half-truths; of things said that are not meant; and fake appearances. When what you see is not what you get, trust can be eroded. So be true to yourself; keep your word; it's a real treasure in these times; it will put you ahead of the pack. In this life, when all else fails, trust is all that remains; it is everything. Without trust, nothing is: not relationships, nor bonds, nor society nor ourselves, nor even tomorrow for when we sleep, we trust tomorrow will come, and with that, we look forward to another crack at the fulfilment of our dreams.

- **The Leverage of being like the eagle:** Observe the masses and do the opposite.

You may not be able to control the flow of time, its apparent scarcity and all, but you can make your own luck with time…and your luck may just be a manifest consequence, a reward, if you like, of things done differently from the crowd. I once saw a poster of an eagle flying above the cloud with rain pouring beneath. You see, the eagle like all birds is not exactly a friend of rain, for personal economic efficiency reasons. Why? It's because a rain-soaked bird has added body weight to deal with in flight. All birds tend to seek physical shelter from the rain to avoid getting wet. The eagle's approach to a solution however, is rather different. What does the eagle do? Rather than be dictated to by the environment and the chaotic scramble for shelter in the confusion of the rainy time of day, the eagle chooses to soar above the cause of the confusion, the clouds. The eagle goes beyond and sits above the clouds where it observes the magnificence of the rain; for the rain is not the enemy. The enemy is the self; it is us who are unprepared in the ways that we ought to have intentionally chosen to act in our best interest. Note that the eagle does not try to manage the rain, nor the clouds that yield it.

The eagle manages the self, its own self, and chooses its acts based on its own plan and self-belief based on its intention to win at life, whatever the cause at stake. How do you defeat a person who has intent to never lose, but to succeed, and to win whatever may befall? Learn from the eagle.

I believe you get the picture. Do not blame Time; do not seek to control or manipulate Time. Do not bemoan Time or curse it nor seek to do other than honour it. You will fail. It is futile. Like the eagle, choose your path. Manage the relationship you have with yourself and with Time, and with it, your very fortune; whatever it may be. You owe it to yourself.

- **The Leverage of choosing to educate yourself:** Self-education is golden. Join knowledge social groups and forums. There are Quora, Thrive Global, Reddit and others. YouTube is awash with many good video programmes. Just choose wisely what you consume. Choose with intention, and choose well. There are many opportunities to learn from other people; people who have been where you are, and are now at the place where you aspire to be. Despite what you may think, many people are generous with tips about what they have learned from their lived experiences and their self-education. All you need to do is ask. Ask with intent to learn, to grow, to be inspired, to aspire to be the very best version of you… because you can achieve it.

Parting shots:

So, there you have it. I trust that with the fore-going pages I have managed to get you to reconsider and start thinking about your time from a slightly different perspective than previously. Indeed, time management is not about time, and its "management" it is about you, and how you and you alone manage yourself, your habits and intentions in relation to what Time you have. Live each moment from a place of INTENTION, a clear intention to extract the optimal amount of good; to make things better, and you will never need to bother, nor worry, about time management, because you will thrive, and to THRIVE is all we are called to do on this side of eternity. Just living is not and has never been enough to progress humanity. If you want to make a difference, seek to thrive and add your own little spark to the glowing STAR of human advancement.

That will be all; and all is enough. Thank you for your interest and attention. **Enjoy your time.**

References

Claudia Hammond, *Time warped: Unlocking the mysteries of time perception*

P WALLISCH, *An odd sense of timing*[1] - Scientific American Mind, 2008 – JSTOR

Siffre, quoted in *Time and trauma*[2]

PG Zimbardo, JN Boyd, *Putting time in perspective*

Stephen Hawking, *A brief history of time: from big bang to black holes.*

---

[1] In the 1930s physiologist Hudson Hoag-and, then at Clark University, hypothesized that a central clock driven by chemical processes in the body could be responsible for this regularity ... attention and memory effects can easily distort the time experience ... The Effect of Predictability.

[2] LC Terr - The Psychoanalytic Study of the Child, 1984 - Taylor & Francis

Chinua Achebe, *Things fall apart*

Jim Loehr, Tony Schwartz, *The power of full engagement: Managing energy, not time, is the key to high performance and personal renewal.*

Phillipa Lally, CHM Van Jaarsveld, *How are habits formed: Modelling habit formation in the real world (European Journal of Social Psychology)*

Kevin Kruse, *15 Secrets Successful people know about Time management: The productivity habits of 7 billionaires, 13 Olympic athletes, 29 straight-A students, and 239 Entrepreneurs.*

LA Seneca, JF Hurst, HC Whiting, *Treatises On Providence, On Tranquillity of Mind, On Shortness of Life, On Happy Life.*

Robert Kiyosaki with Sharon L. Lechter, *Rich Dad's Retire Young, Retire Rich*

Robin Sharma, *(*A YouTube episode) *How to achieve greatness, mastery and enduring fulfilment.*

Jake Knapp and John Zeratsky, *Make Time*

Recommended reading

Steven R. Covey, A. Roger Merrill, and Rebecca R. Merrill, *First Things First*

Francesco Curillo, *The Pomodoro Technique*

Mason Currey, *Daily Rituals*

Hal Elrod, *The Miracle Morning*

Alissa Finerman, *Living in Your Top 1%*

Stephen Guise, *Mini Habits*

Darren Hardy, *The Compound Effect*

Richard Koch, *The 80/20 Principle*

99U and Jocelyn K. Glei, *Manage Your Day-To-Day*

About The Author

Nii Boi-Dsane is a professionally qualified transformative life coach with a special interest in health and retirement coaching. His formal qualifications include a Professional Diploma in Life Coaching with Distinction, a Graduate Diploma in Law, a Master of Arts degree in International Relations, a Post Graduate Diploma in Nursing (Mental Health), a Bachelor of Arts (Honours) degree in Linguistics with English, and a Professional Diploma in Theatre Arts. He is an alumnus of the University of Law and New Bucks University, both in England, and the University of Ghana, Legon.

He enjoys travelling and inter-cultural experiences, and voluntary work. He has been past president of the Rotary eClub of Southern Scotland, District 1020 of Rotary International. Rotary International was founded in February 1905 and is the world's largest voluntary service organization with over one million members in various geographical locations around the globe.

He has previously worked as an actor, writer, theatre producer, broadcaster, teacher, small business owner, corporate executive and an educational consultant. As a life coach, he specializes in helping clients fulfill their lives by aligning their actions with their goals and desires.

His other publications include:
- **Retire Well: A guide to what's important in retirement- Health, Wealth and Relationships**.
- **The Water Principle: How We May Become…**
- **Before the Bell Tolls: Will Your Will do your will? A Guide to your Options in planning your estate.**
- **The Decision Matrix: A Guide To Making Decisions That Serve Your Best Interest.**
- **Reflections: The Art Of Conscious living- An Invitation To Design The Life You desire.**

All are available on Amazon worldwide and at www.self-mastery-books.com

For information regarding how to the author may help you, please see: www.boi-dsane.com

Contact information:

To find out more about how the author can support you, please visit: www.boi-dsane.com

Email: info@boi-dsane.com

www.ingramcontent.com/pod-product-compliance
Lightning Source LLC
Chambersburg PA
CBHW080501220526
45465CB00006B/2343